T0153392

I'M NOT
THAT WOMAN
ANYMORE

I'M NOT THAT WOMAN ANYMORE

A Journey to Healing from Abuse

Dr. Char M. Newbold

Carpenter's Son Publishing

I'm Not That Woman Anymore: A Journey to Healing from Abuse, Leader Guide
© 2021 by Dr. Char M. Newbold

All rights reserved. No part of this book may be reproduced or transmitted in any form or by any means, electronic or mechanical, including photocopying, recording or by any information storage and retrieval system, without permission in writing from the copyright owner.

Scripture quotations marked (AMP) are taken from The Amplified Bible, Old Testament. Copyright © 1965, 1987, by the Zondervan Corporation. Used by permission. All rights reserved.

Amplified Bible, Classic Edition (AMPC)
Used by permission. (www.Lockman.org)

Scripture taken from the NEW AMERICAN STANDARD BIBLE®, Copyright © 1960,1962,1963,1968,1971,1972, 1973,1975,1977,1995 by The Lockman Foundation. Used by permission.

Scripture taken from the Contemporary English Version® Copyright © 1995 American Bible Society. All rights reserved.

Scripture quotations marked HCSB are taken from the Holman Christian Standard Bible®, Copyright © 1999, 2000, 2002, 2003, 2009 by Holman Bible Publishers. Used by permission. Holman Christian Standard Bible®, Holman CSB®, and HCSB® are federally registered trademarks of Holman Bible Publishers.

Easy-to-Read Version. Copyright © 2006 by Bible League international. Used by permission. All rights reserved.

Scripture quotations marked (ESV) are from the ESV® Bible (The Holy Bible, English Standard Version®), copyright © 2001 by Crossway, a publishing ministry of Good News Publishers. Used by permission. All rights reserved.

Good News Translation® (Today's English Version, Second Edition)
Copyright © 1992 American Bible Society. All rights reserved.

Scriptures marked KJV are taken from the KING JAMES VERSION (KJV): public domain.

Scriptures marked (MEV) are taken from the Modern English Version. Copyright © 2014 by Military Bible Association. Used by permission. All rights reserved.
Scripture taken from The Message. Copyright © 1993, 1994, 1995, 1996, 2000, 2001, 2002. Used by permission of NavPress Publishing Group

Scripture quotations marked (NASB) are taken from the New American Standard Bible®, Copyright © 1960, 1962, 1963, 1968, 1971, 1972, 1973, 1975, 1977, 1995 by The Lockman Foundation. Used by permission. (www. Lockman.org)

Scripture quotation from the New Revised Standard Version Bible, copyright © 1989 the Division of Christian Education of the National Council of the Churches of Christ in the United States of America. Used by permission. All rights reserved.

THE NET BIBLE®, NEW ENGLISH TRANSLATION COPYRIGHT (c) 1996 BY BIBLICAL STUDIES PRESS, L.L.C. NET Bible® IS A REGISTERED TRADEMARK THE NET BIBLE® LOGO, SERVICE MARK COPYRIGHT (c) 1997 BY BIBLICAL STUDIES PRESS, L.L.C. ALL RIGHTS RESERVED The NET Bible® is not a shareware program or public domain document and may not be duplicated without permission. For more information, go to http://bible.org/copyright

BIBLE STUDY - LEADER GUIDE

I'M NOT THAT WOMAN ANYMORE

A Journey to Healing from Abuse

Dr. Char M. Newbold

Carpenter's Son Publishing

I'm Not That Woman Anymore: A Journey to Healing from Abuse, Leader Guide
© 2021 by Dr. Char M. Newbold

All rights reserved. No part of this book may be reproduced or transmitted in any form or by any means, electronic or mechanical, including photocopying, recording or by any information storage and retrieval system, without permission in writing from the copyright owner.

Scripture quotations marked (AMP) are taken from The Amplified Bible, Old Testament. Copyright © 1965, 1987, by the Zondervan Corporation. Used by permission. All rights reserved.

Amplified Bible, Classic Edition (AMPC)
Used by permission. (www.Lockman.org)

Scripture taken from the NEW AMERICAN STANDARD BIBLE®, Copyright © 1960,1962,1963,1968,1971,1972, 1973,1975,1977,1995 by The Lockman Foundation. Used by permission.

Scripture taken from the Contemporary English Version® Copyright © 1995 American Bible Society. All rights reserved.

Scripture quotations marked HCSB are taken from the Holman Christian Standard Bible®, Copyright © 1999, 2000, 2002, 2003, 2009 by Holman Bible Publishers. Used by permission. Holman Christian Standard Bible®, Holman CSB®, and HCSB® are federally registered trademarks of Holman Bible Publishers.

Easy-to-Read Version. Copyright © 2006 by Bible League international. Used by permission. All rights reserved.

Scripture quotations marked (ESV) are from the ESV® Bible (The Holy Bible, English Standard Version®), copyright © 2001 by Crossway, a publishing ministry of Good News Publishers. Used by permission. All rights reserved.

Good News Translation® (Today's English Version, Second Edition)
Copyright © 1992 American Bible Society. All rights reserved.

Scriptures marked KJV are taken from the KING JAMES VERSION (KJV): public domain.

Scriptures marked (MEV) are taken from the Modern English Version. Copyright © 2014 by Military Bible Association. Used by permission. All rights reserved.
Scripture taken from The Message. Copyright © 1993, 1994, 1995, 1996, 2000, 2001, 2002. Used by permission of NavPress Publishing Group

Scripture quotations marked (NASB) are taken from the New American Standard Bible®, Copyright © 1960, 1962, 1963, 1968, 1971, 1972, 1973, 1975, 1977, 1995 by The Lockman Foundation. Used by permission. (www.Lockman.org)

Scripture quotation from the New Revised Standard Version Bible, copyright © 1989 the Division of Christian Education of the National Council of the Churches of Christ in the United States of America. Used by permission. All rights reserved.

THE NET BIBLE®, NEW ENGLISH TRANSLATION COPYRIGHT (c) 1996 BY BIBLICAL STUDIES PRESS, L.L.C. NET Bible® IS A REGISTERED TRADEMARK THE NET BIBLE® LOGO, SERVICE MARK COPYRIGHT (c) 1997 BY BIBLICAL STUDIES PRESS, L.L.C. ALL RIGHTS RESERVED The NET Bible® is not a shareware program or public domain document and may not be duplicated without permission. For more information, go to http://bible.org/copyright

Scripture quotations marked (NIV) are taken from the Holy Bible, New International Version®, NIV®. Copyright © 1973, 1978, 1984, 2011 by Biblica, Inc.™ Used by permission of Zondervan. All rights reserved worldwide. www.zondervan.com The "NIV" and "New International Version" are trademarks registered in the United States Patent and Trademark Office by Biblica, Inc.™

Scripture is used from the New King James Version, © 1982 by Thomas Nelson, Inc. All rights reserved. Used by permission.

Scripture quotations are taken from the Holy Bible, New Living Translation, copyright ©1996, 2004, 2007, by Tyndale House Foundation. Used by permission of Tyndale House Publishers, Inc., Carol Stream, Illinois 60188. All rights reserved.

The New Testament in Modern English by J.B Phillips copyright © 1960, 1972 J. B. Phillips. Administered by The Archbishops' Council of the Church of England. Used by Permission.

Scripture quotations marked (TLB) are taken from The Living Bible copyright © 1971. Used by permission of Tyndale House Publishers, Inc., Carol Stream, Illinois 60188. All rights reserved.

Tree of Life (TLV) Translation of the Bible. Copyright © 2015 by The Messianic Jewish Family Bible Society.

The Passion Translation®. Copyright © 2017 by Passion & Fire Ministries, Inc. Used by permission. All rights reserved. thePassionTranslation.com. The Passion Translation® is a registered trademark of Passion & Fire Ministries, Inc.

The Voice Bible Copyright © 2012 Thomas Nelson, Inc. The Voice™ translation © 2012 Ecclesia Bible Society All rights reserved.
Published by Carpenter's Son Publishing, Franklin, Tennessee

Published in association with Larry Carpenter of Christian Book Services, LLC www.christianbookservices.com

Edited by Tiarra Tompkins and Ann Tatlock

Cover and Interior Layout Design by Suzanne Lawing

Printed in the United States of America

978-1-952025-50-1

This Bible study is written by a survivor,
one who has walked through the fire of domestic violence and has come
out not even smelling like smoke because He was and is with me.

It is dedicated to all the women who
have been broken and all those God uses to help.

Note: For the purpose of this work, "survivor" and "victim" will be used interchangeably. Because my experience is almost exclusively with women who have men abusers and because this study is designed for women, the terms "survivor" and "victim" will reference women and "abuser" will reference men. I also have used the terms "domestic violence" and "intimate partner violence" interchangeably.

Although this book focuses on women because women are the majority who suffer in these situations, that is not to negate or downplay the abuse that men also experience with domestic violence. I have known women to be the aggressors and have seen men suffer similar experiences and harm as have the women who have been abused. The survivor stories related within these pages are as I recall them and as they have been shared with me. Many of the survivor stories could be interchangeable with males or females as survivors.

Disclaimer: The sections of this book that contain advice and instruction are meant to be guidelines. There is no replacing proper tools and training for handling small groups or one-on-one domestic violence situations.

MANY THANKS

To my Lord, Jesus Christ: I give my deepest thanks. Without You, I can do nothing.

To my family, church families, and friends: my journey from then until now would have been very different without your prayers, financial support, and love.

To my personal advocates: thank you for lending me your strength when I had none. You share in the victory of every woman who is set free from domestic violence through this work.

To the Purple Posse: you bless me with your incredible strength. You are all amazing!

To my daughter: you have been my biggest motivation to live a safer, healthier life. From your birth, you have offered joy, support, wisdom, and humor. You are my precious gift from God.

To my husband: no one who has encouraged me more than you to finish this writing. Your support has been incredible.

To God be the glory.

Contents

I'M NOT THAT
WOMAN ANYMORE

You can't keep me down anymore
I'm not that woman anymore
No more sorrow, no more shame, no need to try
No, you can't keep me down anymore
You have no power anymore
No more bondage, no more pain
I'm gonna fly

Mr. Prince Charming with your lips full of lies
You wooed me and pursued me all the while in disguise
Your words became cruel, blame and shame took my song
You weren't the man I married; I felt so alone

But you can't keep me down anymore
I'm not that woman anymore
No more sorrow, no more shame, no need to try
No, you can't keep me down anymore
You have no power anymore
No more bondage, no more pain
I'm gonna fly

Crying in the night, curled up afraid to move
You hurt me and destroyed all the love I had for you
Sometimes you cried and tried to make it all right
But you never stopped; your promises were all lies

No, you can't keep me down anymore
I'm not that woman anymore
No more sorrow, no more shame, no need to try
No, you can't keep me down anymore
You have no power anymore
No more bondage, no more pain
I'm gonna fly

And every day I put on my mask. I was fine if anyone asked
Inside I was so empty, the wind could have blown me away
The day came I knew I had to go
My heart broke as I closed the door
All my dreams and hopes and plans
Were stolen from me at the hands of one man

But you can't keep me down anymore
I'm not that woman anymore
No more sorrow, no more shame, no need to try
No, you can't keep me down anymore
You have no power anymore
No more bondage, no more pain
I'm gonna fly

No more sorrow, no more shame
No more bondage, no more pain
I'm gonna fly

Written by Dr. Char Newbold

Introduction

WHY DID I WRITE THIS BIBLE STUDY?

If you read my credentials—a respected teacher, a leader in a local church, a Sunday School teacher, a highly educated woman, an experienced public speaker, and an advocate for children—you wouldn't suspect that I was a victim of domestic violence. If you had asked me then if I was being abused, I would have answered with a resounding, "No!" Why? Because I did not believe I was. On my honest days, I would have said my husband had a drinking problem or anger issues. The common misconception about abuse is it means "he hits you." He never broke any bones or put me in the hospital, so he would have told you he wasn't abusive either. Truthfully, he treated me better than his dad treated his mom.

Having grown up in an upper-middle-class neighborhood with two loving parents who raised me in church and never resorted to violent behavior in the home, I had no experience with abusive behavior. If you had asked me what an abusive relationship looked like, I would have given you the same cliché we've seen in the movies for decades: the bruised and battered wife unable or unwilling to leave her marriage. I was a married Christian with a good job, a beautiful child, and close friends. I couldn't be a victim of domestic violence—yet I was.

Only with the help of domestic violence advocates and a support group for victims did I begin to understand that my former husband exhibited the behavior of an abuser. Worse, I exhibited the behavior of a victim. This realization didn't come easily. Because he never raised his hand to hit me and I didn't have to explain away frequent injuries, I was in denial about his abuse. With time, I came to realize I had been abused in more ways than one. The physical, emotional, financial, and even sexual abuse had gone on longer than I had realized. The once subtle signs I had brushed off were now glaring. With the recognition of abuse often comes shame and blame. I gradually learned to switch my thinking from blaming myself and continually trying to fix our relationship to understanding that I was not responsible for his behavior nor solely responsible for improving our marriage. I also came to understand that I deserved a better life than the one I had with him. With the additional help of my supportive family and friends, I grew to believe in my value as a woman and as a child of God. Encouraged, I grew closer to Him and drew my strength from Him.

> *It is God who arms me with strength and*
> *makes my way perfect. Psalm 18:32 NKJV*

As with any major life event, everyone has an opinion about what is right and wrong. Along the way, misguided, uninformed faith leaders and fellow Christians gave me a variety of bad counsel. I am so grateful for the divine appointment leading me to the man of God who correctly counseled me spiritually while I was still in my relationship, every time I left, and after I left for good. He taught me to study the Word and develop the ability to hear God for myself. As I began to understand the truth of God's Word and His love for me, I gained the courage to leave and the grace to heal. Thanks, Pastor.

Let the Church arise as a beacon of hope.

I now consider myself a survivor and a thriver, not a victim. Yes, bad things happened to me, but I don't let them define who I am now. In the later stages of my journey to wholeness, God spoke to me about helping others.

> *Speak up for those who cannot speak for themselves;*
> *ensure justice for those being crushed. Yes, speak up for the*
> *poor and helpless, and see that they get justice. Proverbs 31:8-9 NLT*

This Bible study is part of my obedience to Him. My sincere prayer is that through these pages, the women who come to the faith community for help will experience the heart of God for those being crushed. And as His servants, let us minister to the spiritual, physical, and emotional needs of those affected by domestic violence who seek our help, from first disclosure to extended care. Let the Church arise as a beacon of hope.

"For I know the plans and thoughts that I have for you,"
says the LORD, "plans for peace and well-being and not for disaster,
to give you a future and a hope." Jeremiah 29:11 AMP

Welcome

I want to thank you for choosing *I'm Not That Woman Anymore* Bible study. These 12 lessons are written specifically for women affected by domestic violence whether it is your partner or spouse. I use them with one of the support groups I facilitate.

There is no suggested length of time to complete this study. Healing takes time. You may need to repeat some lessons, and that's okay. Healing is a process. While the lessons are designed to build on each other, they do not have to be completed in order. I have provided lines on which to record your answers, but don't feel pressured to fill up every one. I prefer to err on the side of giving too much space to write instead of too little.

It is possible that some of the lessons, activities, or survivor stories may awaken flashbacks or memories of traumatic events. Please stop and take care of yourself if you feel overwhelmed with emotions or begin to feel upset, fearful, uncomfortable, confused, or anxious. It's okay to take a break or skip a lesson for a while. You may want to complete the painful or distressing parts with a trusted friend or family member. If you prefer, you may also call the National Domestic Violence Hotline at (800) 799-7233 to find advocates near you who can listen and help you process what has happened to you. I'm also a fan of talking to experienced trauma-trained counselors or therapists who specialize in working with those harmed or affected by violence in the home. It is essential for your well-being to connect with others who can help and not stay isolated in your distress.

If you are still struggling to understand the complex dynamics of domestic violence, you may find another book I wrote, *The Church's Response to Domestic Violence*, helpful. This book contains information I have learned from years of research, training, and advocacy that would be helpful to you. I also have included a few resources at the back of this Bible study. If you need specific help your church may not offer, I encourage you to contact domestic violence organizations and advocates in your area to provide information, resources, and support.

The purple butterfly on the cover is the perfect image of how many survivors feel after getting free from the prison of abuse. Purple is the color of domestic violence awareness, and the butterfly represents the metamorphosis from dark captivity to fluttering freely in the Light. I pray such transformation occurs for countless women through this Bible study. By the end, I hope that each of you can genuinely say, "I'm not that woman anymore."

God bless you,

Dr. Char

drchar.nbb@gmail.com

Lesson 1

HEAVENLY LOVE

You have turned for me my mourning into dancing; You have put off
my sackcloth and clothed me with gladness. Psalm 30:11 NKJV

One of my greatest joys is watching women who have been horribly mistreated blossom as they come to know the love of God. The lies of the enemy they have believed through the words and actions of their abusers lose power as the love of God is revealed and overcomes the abuse. Joy is restored, or perhaps experienced for the first time, as the love of God becomes a tangible presence in their lives. The survivors I know liken this transformation to that of becoming a butterfly after having been trapped in a cocoon.

What better way to start our journey together than with a letter from our Abba Father. In His letter, His love for us is clear. It is my prayer that you will absorb into your innermost being the words God speaks to you through His Word. Take note of those things He says that particularly resonate with you. They are all found in Scripture. Meditate on them, and commit them to memory.

If your relationship with God has suffered because of your abuse, today can be the first step in coming closer to Him as He draws you with His love. Dare to lean in and let Him whisper His love in your ears. Dare to hear the song He sings over you. Dare to open yourself up to love from the greatest source ever!

ACTIVITY: Watch the following video:
https://www.fathersloveletter.com/video.html [1]

I prefer the 2014 version. It takes about 6 minutes. A copy of the script and the Scriptures used are below.

My Child,

You may not know Me, but I know everything about you.[(1)] *I know when you sit down and when you rise up.*[(2)] *I am familiar with all your ways*[(3)] *Even the very hairs on your head are numbered*[(4)] *For you were made in My image.*[(5)] *In Me you live and move and have your being, for you are My offspring.*[(6)] *I knew you even before you were conceived.*[(7)] *I chose you when I planned creation.*[(8)] *You were not a mistake, for all your days are written in My book.* [(9)] *I determined the exact time of your birth and where you would live.*[(10)] *You are fearfully and wonderfully made.*[(11)] *I knit you together in your mother's womb*[(12)] *And brought you forth on the day you were born.*[(13)] *I have been misrepresented by those who don't know Me.*[(14)] *I am not distant and angry, but am the complete expression of love.*[(15)] *And it is My desire to lavish My love on you simply because you are My child and I am your Father.*[(16)] *I offer you more than your earthly father ever could*[(17)] *For I am the perfect Father.*[(18)] *Every good gift that you receive comes from My hand*[(19)] *For I am your provider and I meet all your needs.*[(20)] *My plan for your future has always been filled with hope.*[(21)] *Because I love you with an everlasting love,*[(22)] *My thoughts toward you are countless as the sand on the seashore*[(23)] *And I rejoice over you with singing.*[(24)] *I will never stop doing good to you*[(25)] *For you are My treasured possession.*[(26)] *I desire to establish you with all My heart and all My soul*[(27)] *And I want to show you great and marvelous things.*[(28)] *If you seek Me with all your heart, you will find Me.*[(29)] *Delight in Me and I will give you the desires of your heart*[(30)] *For it is I who gave you those desires.*[(31)] *I am able to do more for you than you could possibly imagine*[(32)] *For I am your greatest encourager.*[(33)] *I am also the Father who comforts you in all your troubles.* [(34)] *When you are brokenhearted, I am close to you.*[(35)] *As a shepherd carries a lamb, I have carried you close to My heart.*[(36)] *One day I will wipe away every tear from your eyes. And I'll take away all the pain you have suffered on this earth.*[(37)] *I am your Father, and I love you even as I love my Son, Jesus.*[(38)] *For in Jesus, My love for you is revealed.*[(39)] *He is the exact representation of My being.*[(40)] *He came to demonstrate that I am for you, not against you*[(41)] *And to tell you that I am not counting your sins. Jesus died so that you and I could be reconciled.* [(42)] *His death was the ultimate expression of My love for you.*[(43)] *I gave up everything I loved that I might gain your love.*[(44)] *If you receive the gift of My Son Jesus, you receive Me*[(45)] *And nothing will ever separate you from My love again.*[46] *Come home and I'll throw the biggest party heaven has ever seen.*[47] *I have always been Father and will always be Father.*[48] *My question is... Will you be My child?*[49] *I am waiting for you.*[50]

Love, Your Dad.
Almighty God

Father's Love Letter is a compilation of the following paraphrased Bible verses presented in the form of a love letter from God to you. Here are the Scriptures used.

(1) Psalm 139:1; (2) Psalm 139:2; (3) Psalm 139:3; (4) Matthew 10:29-31; (5) Genesis 1:27; (6) Acts 17:28; (7) Jeremiah 1:4-5; (8) Ephesians 1:11-12; (9) Psalm 139:15-16; (10) Acts 17:26; (11) Psalm 139:14; (12) Psalm 139:13; (13) Psalm 71:6; (14) John 8:41-44; (15) 1 John 4:16; (16) 1 John 3:1; (17) Matthew 7:11; (18) Matthew 5:48; (19) James 1:17; (20) Matthew 6:31-33; (21) Jeremiah 29:11; (22) Jeremiah 31:3; (23) Psalm 139:17-18; (24) Zephaniah 3:17; (25) Jeremiah 32:40; (26) Exodus 19:5; (27) Jeremiah 32:41; (28) Jeremiah 33:3; (29) Deuteronomy 4:29; (30) Psalm 37:4; (31) Philippians 2:13; (32) Ephesians 3:20; (33) 2 Thessalonians 2:16-17; (34) 2 Corinthians 1:3-4; (35) Psalm 34:18; (36) Isaiah 40:11; (37) Revelation 21:3-4; (38) John 17:23; (39) John 17:26; (40) Hebrews 1:3; (41) Romans 8:31; (42) 2 Corinthians 5:18-19; (43) 1 John 4:10; (44) Romans 8:31-32; (45) 1 John 2:23; (46) Romans 8:38-39; (47) Luke 15:7; (48) Ephesians 3:14-15; (49) John 1:12-13; (50) Luke 15:11-32.

> **Survivor**: One Sunday after one of the times I left my abuser, I was at church. During worship, the Lord spoke to me (in my mind). He said, "Daughter, I am pleased." I was stunned! God was pleased with me? Here I was separated from my husband, mentally and physically a wreck, barely making it through each day, and God calls me, "Daughter," and tells me He is pleased? I was overwhelmed with emotion. God was pleased with me despite the mess in my life. For the very first time, I had a glimpse of just how much He loves me. I've never been the same.

JOURNAL

Write down which statements in the letter from God are easiest for you to believe and accept. Then write the ones hardest for you to believe and accept. Think about reasons why some are easier for you than others to accept as truth.

PRAYER

Abba, thank You for loving me. I have been so hurt and wounded; it is hard for me to trust that perfect love such as Yours exists. Help me to receive Your love. Let it fill all the places in me that are empty. Soak me in Your love now and in the days ahead. In the loving name of Jesus I pray, Amen.

Heavenly Love Activity

DECORATED LETTER

MATERIALS NEEDED:

- 1 copy of the Father's Love Letter located at
  https://www.fathersloveletter.com/text.html

- Colored markers or pencils

- One picture frame with a hanger or stand that holds an 8.5 x 11 paper (optional)

DIRECTIONS:

1. Print a copy of the Father's Love Letter.

2. Draw and color a border along the sides of the letter.

3. Place the letter in the frame. (optional)

My Child,

You may not know Me, but I know everything about you. I know when you sit down and when you rise up. I am familiar with all your ways. Even the very hairs on your head are numbered. For you were made in My image. In Me you live and move and have your being. For you are My offspring. I knew you even before you were conceived. I chose you when I planned creation. You were not a mistake, for all your days are written in My book. I determined the exact time of your birth and where you would live. You are fearfully and wonderfully made. I knit you together in your mother's womb. And brought you forth on the day you were born. I have been misrepresented by those who don't know Me. I am not distant and angry, but am the complete expression of love. And it is my desire to lavish My love on you. Simply because you are my child and I am your Father. I offer you more than your earthly father ever could. For I am the perfect father. Every good gift that you receive comes from My hand. For I am your provider and I meet all your needs. My plan for your future has always been filled with hope. Because I love you with an everlasting love. My thoughts toward you are countless as the sand on the seashore. And I rejoice over you with singing. I will never stop doing good to you. For you are My treasured possession. I desire to establish you with all My heart and all My soul. And I want to show you great and marvelous things. If you seek Me with all your heart, you will find me. Delight My son, Jesus. For in Jesus, My love for you is revealed. He is the I loved that I might gain your love. If you receive the gift of My son Jesus, you receive me. And nothing will ever separate you from My love again. Come home and I'll throw the biggest party heaven has ever seen. I have always been Father, and will always be Father. My question is ... Will you be My child? I am waiting for you.

Love, Your Dad

Lesson 2

WHO AM I?

But as many as received Him, to them He gave the right to
become children of God, even to those who believe in His name.
John 1:12 NKJV

Who you are is important to God. What you do with your life is important to God. It is no accident you are here. Just as with Esther, He planned where He wanted you to be right now.

For if you keep silent at this time, relief and deliverance will rise for the Jews from
another place, but you and your father's house will perish. And who knows whether you
have not come to the kingdom for such a time as this? Esther 4:14 ESV

Our identities come from our earthly parents. Our identities as Christians come from our heavenly Father. We saw in the last lesson how much He loves us. Once we follow Christ, our identity changes. Our daddy is The King, and we become royalty having all the benefits as The King's beloved child. The enemy wants to keep us from understanding our identity in Christ. It is critical we know who we are so we can't be shaken by the words of an abuser or unkind person.

Survivor: The first time my abuser called me a horrible name and accused me of horrible things, I was shocked. I had never heard anyone called such a vile thing. I was terrified because he was so angry. I was hurt because these cruel words were coming out of the mouth of the man who claimed to love me. I was confused because I had no idea where all this ugliness was coming from. When my abuser would call me horrible names and accuse me of doing horrible things, I knew they weren't true. I wasn't that person he was describing. I would try to explain that I wasn't like that; I wouldn't do that. I would plead with him to tell me what I had done that would make him think such a thing. I would apologize for anything he said I had done to make him think such things. I would reassure him of my faithfulness. I would tell him over and over that I loved him and would never do those things he accused me of doing. I would promise to try harder. By the time he was done, I was a hysterical, sobbing mess. I was beaten by his words.

Let's look more closely at who God says you are.

1. As a child of God, I am _____

_____.

> *The Spirit Himself bears witness with our spirit that*
> *we are children of God, and if children, then heirs—*
> *heirs of God and joint heirs with Christ…. Romans 8:16-17 NKJV*

2. I am _____.

> *Therefore, if anyone is in Christ, he is a new creation; old things have passed away;*
> *behold, all things have come new. 2 Corinthians 5:17 NKJV*

3. I am _____.

> *I praise you because I am fearfully and wonderfully made;*
> *your works are wonderful, I know that full well. Psalm 139:14 NIV*

4. I am _____.

> *And to put on the new self, created after the likeness of God*
> *in true righteousness and holiness. Ephesians 4:24 ESV*

5. I am _____.

Keep me as the apple of your eye; hide me in the
shadow of your wings. Psalm 17:8 NIV

6. I am _____.

No, in all these things we are more than conquerors
through him who loved us. Romans 8:37 NIV

7. I can _____
_____.

I can do all things through Christ who strengthens me. Philippians 4:13 NKJV

8. I have been chosen of God, and I am _____.

So, as those who have been chosen of God, holy and beloved, put on a heart of
compassion, kindness, humility, gentleness and patience. Colossians 3:12 NASB

9. I am _____.

Knowing, brethren beloved by God, His choice of you. 1 Thessalonians 1:4 NASB

10. I am _____
_____.

Just as He chose us in Him before the foundation of the world,
that we would be holy and blameless before Him. Ephesians 1:4 NASB

11. I am _____.

No longer do I call you slaves, for the slave does not know what his master
is doing; but I have called you friends, for all things that I have heard from
My Father I have made known to you. John 15:15 NASB

12. I am_____
_____.

But you are a chosen generation, a royal priesthood, a holy nation,
His own special people, that you may proclaim the praises of Him
who called you out of darkness into His marvelous light. 1 Peter 2:9 NKJV

13. I am _____

_____

as I heed (give careful attention to) His commandments and observe (obey) them.

And the Lord will make you the head and not the tail; you shall be above only, and not be beneath, if you heed the commandments of the Lord your God, which I command you today, and are careful to observe them. Deuteronomy 28:13 NKJV

14. I am _____.

Being justified freely by His grace through the redemption that is in Christ Jesus. Romans 3:24 NKJV

15. I am _____.

Knowing this, that our old man was crucified with Him, that the body of sin might be done away with, that we would no longer be slaves to sin. Romans 6:6 NKJV

16. I am _____.

Therefore there is now no condemnation to those who are in Christ Jesus, who do not walk according to the flesh, but according to the Spirit. Romans 8:1 NKJV

17. I am _____.

Accept one another, then, just as Christ accepted you, in order to bring praise to God. Romans 15:7 NIV

18. In Christ Jesus, I am _____

_____.

But of Him you are in Christ Jesus, who became for us wisdom from God—and righteousness and sanctification and redemption. 1 Corinthians 1:30 NKJV

19. My body is _____

_____.

Do you not know that you are the temple of God and that the Spirit of God dwells in you? 1 Corinthians 3:16 NKJV

20. I am _____

_____.

But he who is joined to the Lord is one spirit with Him. 1 Corinthians 6:17 NKJV

21. I am _____

_____.

For He made Him who knew no sin to be sin for us, that we might become the righteousness of God in Him. 2 Corinthians 5:21 NKJV

22. I am no longer a slave, but _____ and an heir of God.

So you are no longer a slave, but God's child; and since you are his child, God has made you also an heir. Galatians 4:7 NIV

23. I am _____.

It is for freedom that Christ has set us free. Galatians 5:1 NIV

24. I am _____

_____.

Praise be to the God and Father of our Lord Jesus Christ, who has blessed us in the heavenly realms with every spiritual blessing in Christ. Ephesians 1:3 NIV

25. I am _____

_____.

In him you also were sealed with the promised Holy Spirit when you heard the word of truth, the gospel of your salvation, and when you believed. Ephesians 1:13 CSB

26. I am _____

_____.

And God raised us up with Christ and seated us with him in the heavenly realms in Christ Jesus. Ephesians 2:6 NIV

27. I am _____

_____.

> *For we are God's masterpiece. He has created us*
> *anew in Christ Jesus, so we can do the good things*
> *he planned for us long ago. Ephesians 2:10 NLT*

28. I am _____

_____.

> *In whom we have boldness and access with confidence*
> *through faith in Him. Ephesians 3:12 ESV*

29. I was formerly darkness, but now I am _____

_____.

> *For you were once darkness, but now you are light in the Lord.*
> *Walk as children of light. Ephesians 5:8 NKJV*

30. I am _____.

> *And you are complete in Him, who is the head of all*
> *principality and power. Colossians 2:10 NKJV*

Oh, if we could ever grab hold of our identity in Christ and never let the enemy overshadow who we are and who we belong to! Gone would be our insecurities, our shame, our guilt, or feelings of unworthiness. Gone would be anyone's ability to have us believe anything different. We are royalty made in the image of the Creator of the Universe who chose us. He calls us His masterpiece. That alone is enough to get us excited!

JOURNAL

Write your three favorite truths that you read in this lesson. How will you apply these truths to your life?

PRAYER

Heavenly Father, how grateful I am to get my identity from You. Help me to accept Your idea of who I am instead of my own. I choose right now to view myself as You view me. When I look in the mirror, I will see Your image of me instead of the one I have believed. Help me to release the lies of the enemy that I have falsely accepted about who

I am. Help me believe deep within myself that I am who You say I am. Help me to be so rooted in who You say I am that I cannot and will not be shaken by the hurtful words of man. Thank You, Father. In the majestic name of Jesus I pray, Amen.

Who Am I? Activity

WORD CLOUDS

MATERIALS NEEDED:

• Computer with internet connection

• An email address to send the word cloud for printing

• *The Name Book* by Dorothy Astoria ©1982, 1997 from Bethany House Publishers

• Computer paper (I like to use a fancier marble paper.)

• A list of words or short phrases describing who God says you are

DIRECTIONS:

1. Find your name in *The Name Book*. Write down the inherent meaning and spiritual connotation.

2. On your computer, go to https://worditout.com/word-cloud/create

3. On the left side of the screen, select normal text.

4. Type your words in the box that says ORIGINAL TEXT.
   a. First, type your name in the box five (5) times using a capital for the first letter and placing a space between each name. By typing your name five times, your name will appear in the largest font.
   b. Second, type the inherent meaning of your name and the spiritual connotation three (3) times in the box following your name. If there is a phrase, begin each word in the phrase with a capital letter but do not use spaces between the words in the phrase. Do place a space between phrases. These words will appear in the second largest font.
   c. Next, type in the words and phrases you wrote describing who God says you are. Start each new word with a capital letter and each word in a phrase with a capital letter. You should type these words just once. Again, avoid adding spaces in between words in a phrase, but do leave a space between single words and between each phrase.

5. When you have typed in all your words, select GENERATE. You will be shown your word cloud.

6. Continue clicking REGENERATE on the left side until you find the word cloud you would like to print. Click save to your email. You may want to create a separate email account.

7. Your word cloud will be sent to the email you selected where it can be downloaded and printed.

Here is simplified example of how it will look.

Kindness   *Accepted*
Masterpiece

Loved   *Char*   *Strong*

Forgiven   *Wonderfully Made*

Blessed   *Righteous*   *New Creation*

Chosen   *Free*   *Virtuous*

Lesson 3

SCRIPTURE TWISTING

Be diligent to present yourself approved to God,
a worker who does not need to be ashamed,
rightly dividing the word of truth.
2 Timothy 2:15 NKJV

Survivor: The incredible power of faith has enabled so many women to take a stand against abuse in their families. I didn't have that kind of faith the first several years of my married life to my abuser. In fact, I did not have much understanding of Scripture, never having truly studied it for myself. My knowledge primarily came from Sunday sermons and the occasional Bible study. I believed what I was told.

The worse things got at home, the more I devoured counseling and self-help books searching for the answers. Just tell me what steps to take, what formula to use, what changes to make. I read my Bible more and prayed more, looking for answers. I didn't understand how a loving God would not answer my prayers to change this man who so obviously had problems. How could God not answer my prayers to protect my family and me? I felt disloyal and disrespectful talking about my husband to others. I was timid about reaching out to spiritually mature Christians for scriptural understanding; I didn't want to look stupid. I didn't want to be criticized or judged for telling the truth about my marriage.

The few times I tentatively reached out, the answers I got didn't seem to fit my situation. "Submit, turn the other cheek, forgive 70 times 7, go the extra mile, iron sharpens iron, a kind word turns away wrath, if an unsaved man wants to stay let him stay, God hates divorce, perfect love casts out fear, we all fall short of the glory of God, look at the plank in your own eye before dealing with the splinter in his, you without sin cast the first stone, pray fervently, fast." I did submit; he didn't change. I did turn the other cheek; he didn't change. I did forgive way more than 490 times; he didn't change. I did go the extra mile lots and lots of times; he didn't change. I cried out to God to show me my sins and remove my rough edges; he didn't change. I offered kind words and words of encouragement; he didn't change. I refused to consider divorce and told him I wouldn't ever leave; he didn't change. I cried out to God to help me love him as He loved him; he didn't change. I admitted my sins in our relationship to him and asked his forgiveness for my shortcomings; he didn't change. I was constantly rooting out my own sin and working to be a better person and a better wife; he didn't change. I prayed continual, impassioned prayers for God to stop the bad stuff; he didn't change. I fasted; he didn't change.

I questioned if God was punishing me for my past sins. I questioned what I was doing wrong as a Christian. I questioned if God was real. I questioned if He even cared. The problem was I was trying to deal with my abuser's outer surface issues of alcohol, drugs, anger, control, manipulation, selfishness, violence, and infidelity when the problem was his sinful inner heart attitude. I was trying to impose my will over his free will. Abuse was his choice.

There is only One who can change hearts. When God becomes part of our lives, we are changed from the inside out. It is through the power of the Holy Spirit, the Word of God, and through prayer that our hearts and lives are changed. That means the abuser is responsible for his own heart attitude based on his relationship with God. No change can occur in his behavior until there is a heart transformation inside him. Everything I was doing to get him to change was ineffective. I couldn't rescue him. I couldn't change him. I couldn't transform his heart. I wasn't his Savior—only Jesus is. "And I will give you a new heart, and a new spirit I will put within you. And I will remove the heart of stone from your flesh and give you a heart of flesh. And I will put my Spirit within you, and cause you to walk in my statutes and be careful to obey my rules." (Ezekiel 36:26-27 ESV)

In time, I changed churches and began to learn about who God really is and about His true nature and character. I learned that He is good and wants good things for me. I learned how to research the Scriptures myself and how to hear God for myself. I was blessed with people in my life who also knew how to hear from God who encouraged me and confirmed what I was hearing and learning. I discovered books, teachings, and ministries that helped me understand what the Word of God is really saying. It was primarily up to me to rightly divide the Word of truth revealed by the Holy Spirit as it applied to my personal situation. I sought His peace about my decisions.

THE ENEMY REVEALED

Who does Scripture say is really our enemy?

1. The devil is a _____. He is the _____.

   You are of your father the devil, and the desires of your father you want to do.
   He was a murderer from the beginning, and does not stand in the truth,
   because there is no truth in him. When he speaks a lie, he speaks from
   his own resources, for he is a liar and the father of it. John 8:44 NKJV

2. We are warned to watch out for our _____, the
   devil who wants to _____ us.

   Be sober, be vigilant; because your adversary the devil walks about
   like a roaring lion, seeking whom he may devour. 1 Peter 5:8 NKJV

3. The enemy wants us to believe his perverted, twisted version of the truth. He's smart enough to include a bit of truth but twists the meaning or application of the Scripture just as he did with _____ in the garden.

Now the serpent was more cunning than any beast of the field which the Lord God had made. And he said to the woman, "Has God indeed said, 'You shall not eat of every tree of the garden'?" And the woman said to the serpent, "We may eat the fruit of the trees of the garden; but of the fruit of the tree which is in the midst of the garden, God has said, 'You shall not eat it, nor shall you touch it, lest you die.'" Then the serpent said to the woman, "You will not surely die. For God knows that in the day you eat of it your eyes will be opened, and you will be like God, knowing good and evil." So when the woman saw that the tree was good for food, that it was pleasant to the eyes, and a tree desirable to make one wise, she took of its fruit and ate. She also gave to her husband with her, and he ate. Then the eyes of both of them were opened, and they knew that they were

naked; and they sewed fig leaves together and made themselves coverings.
Genesis 3:1-7 NKJV

4. God had never said touching the tree would cause death. I imagine when Eve touched the tree and didn't die, she figured the devil was telling the truth. He had her hooked then. It was a small step to get her to believe his lie, "You will be like God." The enemy pounced on Eve's _____
about what God actually said just as he does with us today.

The Lord God took the man and put him in the garden of Eden to work it and keep it. And the Lord God commanded the man, saying, "You may surely eat of every tree of the garden, but of the tree of the knowledge of good and evil you shall not eat, for in the day that you eat of it you shall surely die." Genesis 2:15-17 ESV

By searching the Scriptures and correctly applying the Word by focusing on what God actually says about abuse, we are no longer prey to the enemy's Scripture-twisting because we know the truth. When you know that you know that you know the truth, you can stand firm on His Word and not be moved by the words of your abuser, well-meaning friends and family, and even misinformed Christians.

It's up to us to study the Scriptures and rightly divide the truth from the lies.

SCRIPTURAL TRUTHS ABOUT ABUSE

1. What does God say about abusers? His soul _____ the one who loves violence. They will not inherit _____. They stir up _____ and commit many _____.

The Lord tests the righteous, but His soul hates the wicked
and the one who loves violence. Psalm 11:5 ESV

The acts of the flesh are obvious: sexual immorality, impurity and debauchery; idolatry and witchcraft; hatred, discord, jealousy, fits of rage, selfish ambition, dissensions, factions and envy; drunkenness, orgies, and the like. I warn you, as I did before, that those who live like this will not inherit the kingdom of God. Galatians 5:19-21 NIV

An angry person stirs up conflict, and a hot-tempered person
commits many sins. Proverbs 29:22 NIV

2. What does God say to put way? He says to put away _____

_____

_____.

*Let all bitterness and wrath and anger and clamor and slander be put
away from you, along with all malice. Ephesians 4:31 ESV*

*But now you must put them all away: anger, wrath, malice, slander,
and obscene talk from your mouth. Colossians 3:8 ESV*

3. How does God expect us to treat one another? We are to _____

_____.

*A new commandment I give to you, that you love one another:
just as I have loved you, you also are to love one another. John 13:34 ESV*

4. What is God's plan for those of us facing violence? God _____

_____ from violence.

*Let those who love the Lord hate evil, for he guards the lives
of his faithful one and delivers them from the hand of the wicked. Psalm 97:10 NIV*

*My God, my rock, in whom I take refuge, my shield,
and the horn of my salvation, my stronghold and my refuge,
my savior; you save me from violence. 2 Samuel 22:3 ESV*

5. How does God feel about us being around abusers? He _____

_____.

He wants us to _____ from danger.

*Do not envy the wicked, do not desire their company;
for their hearts plot violence, and their lips talk
about making trouble. Proverbs 24:1-2 NIV*

*Do not make friends with a hot-tempered person,
do not associate with one easily angered. Proverbs 22:24 NIV*

*People will be lovers of themselves, lovers of money, boastful, proud, abusive, disobedient
to their parents, ungrateful, unholy, without love, unforgiving, slanderous, without*

self-control, brutal, not lovers of the good, treacherous, rash, conceited, lovers of pleasure rather than lovers of God—having a form of godliness but denying its power. Have nothing to do with such people. 2 Timothy 3:2-5 NIV

The prudent see danger and hide, but the naïve keep going and pay the penalty. Proverbs 27:12 TLV

6. A marriage relationship has expectations for both spouses. Violence and abuse have no place in a marriage. What are God's expectations for husbands? God expects husbands to _____

_____

_____

_____

_____.

Just as Christ never causes us hurt or shame, so should a husband never cause his wife hurt or shame.

Husbands, love your wives, just as Christ also loved the church and gave Himself for her, that He might sanctify and cleanse her with the washing of water by the word, that He might present her to Himself a glorious church, not having spot or wrinkle or any such thing, but that she should be holy and without blemish. So husbands ought to love their own wives as their own bodies; he who loves his wife loves himself. For no one ever hated his own flesh, but nourishes and cherishes it, just as the Lord does the church. Ephesians 5:25-29 NKJV

Husbands, love your wives, and do not be harsh with them. Colossians 3:19 ESV

7. What are God's expectations for wives? God expects wives to _____

_____

_____ just as the husband submits to Christ. "What is described here is a model based on Christ's relationship to the church: Jesus was the servant of all who followed him and he gave himself up for them. Never did he order people around, threaten, hit, or frighten them."[2]

Nevertheless let each one of you in particular so love his own wife as himself, and let the wife see that she respects her husband. Ephesians 5:33 NKJV

Wives, submit to your husbands, as is fitting in the Lord. Colossians 3:18 ESV

8. What should wives expect to receive from their mates besides love? Wives are to receive _____.

They also should receive _____ as a fellow heir of Christ.

In the same way, you husbands, live with your wives in an understanding way [with great gentleness and tact, and with an intelligent regard for the marriage relationship], as with someone physically weaker, since she is a woman. Show her honor and respect as a fellow heir of the grace of life, so that your prayers will not be hindered or ineffective.
1 Peter 3:7 AMP

9. Who is responsible for peacefulness in the home? _____

is responsible for peacefulness in the home.

Because everyone will do what is right, there will be peace and security forever. God's people will be free from worries, and their homes peaceful and safe.
Isaiah 32:17-18 GNT

Know this, my beloved brothers: let every person be quick to hear, slow to speak, slow to anger. James 1:19 ESV

Read the following Scriptures.

But to you who are willing to listen, I say, love your enemies! Do good to those who hate you. Bless those who curse you. Pray for those who hurt you. If someone slaps you on one cheek, offer the other cheek also. If someone demands your coat, offer your shirt also.
Luke 6:27-29 NLT

You have heard that it was said, "An eye for an eye, and a tooth for a tooth [punishment that fits the offense]." But I say to you, do not resist an evil person [who insults you or violates your rights]; but whoever slaps you on the right cheek, turn the other toward him also [simply ignore insignificant insults or trivial losses and do not bother to retaliate—maintain your dignity, your self-respect, your poise]. Matthew 5:38-39 AMP

A spouse or other family member is not supposed to be your enemy!

Jesus speaks here against seeking vengeance or escalating violence between enemies in legal cases.[3] A spouse or other family member is not supposed to be your enemy! When another's violence does not stop, the only way you can prevent further escalation is leaving the situation. You can pray for an abuser without subjecting yourself to continued abuse. By leaving, you are helping the abuser not to sin. By leaving, you are protecting the children God placed in your care.

10. Explain the concept of turning the other cheek. _____
_____
_____
_____.

11. All of our emotions have a purpose. For example, pain alerts us that something is wrong in our body. Fear also alerts us that something is wrong. If we are in a dangerous or potentially harmful situation, our fear causes the brain to send signals to our body to act. You've probably heard of your body's natural reactions to intense fear by fighting back (fight response), fleeing (flight response), shutting down (freeze response), or appeasing/pleasing (fawn response). This kind of fear is healthy and helpful in keeping us safe. There is another kind of fear. This fear prevents us from having a joyful life full of purpose and victory. It torments us by taking over our hearts and minds. It is not based in reality but can find its roots in trauma such as abuse.

God wants us to be free of harmful fear.

What does God say about this harmful fear? _____
_____
_____.

These Scriptures are not saying you should be unwise regarding your safety.

For God has not given us a spirit of fear, but of power and of love and of a sound mind.
2 Timothy 1:7 NKJV

Out of my distress I called on the Lord; the Lord answered me and set me free. The Lord is on my side; I will not fear. What can man do to me? The Lord is on my side as my helper; I shall look in triumph on those who hate me. Psalm 118:5-7 ESV

The fear of human opinion disables; trusting in God
protects you from that. Proverbs 29:25 MSG

12. Abuse is not voluntary. It does not bring glory to God because it is not the will of God; it is the selfish will of the abuser. God does not bless suffering because of abuse. What kind of persecution does bring God glory? We are blessed when we are voluntarily persecuted for the _____

_____ which brings glory to God.

"Blessed are those who are persecuted for righteousness' sake, for theirs is the kingdom of heaven. "Blessed are you when others revile you and persecute you and utter all kinds of evil against you falsely on my account. Rejoice and be glad, for your reward is great in heaven, for so they persecuted the prophets who were before you. Matthew 5:10-12 ESV

But even if you should suffer for righteousness' sake, you will be blessed.
Have no fear of them, nor be troubled. 1 Peter 3:14 ESV

Read the following Scriptures about divorce. You may have heard that God does not sanction divorce; however, God divorced Israel who was unwilling to keep their commitment to Him or obey His commandments.

The Lord said also to me in the days of Josiah the king: "Have you seen what backsliding Israel has done? She has gone up on every high mountain and under every green tree, and there played the harlot. And I said, after she had done all these things, 'Return to Me.' But she did not return. And her treacherous sister Judah saw it. Then I saw that for all the causes for which backsliding Israel had committed adultery, I had put her away and given her a certificate of divorce; yet her treacherous sister Judah did not fear, but went and played the harlot also. So it came to pass, through her casual harlotry, that she defiled the land and committed adultery with stones and trees. And yet for all this her treacherous sister Judah has not turned to Me with her whole heart, but in pretense," says the Lord. Jeremiah 3:6-10 NKJV

In Malachi, the divorce practice God hated was a husband's disregard for the marriage covenant when he divorced his wife for no real reason other than he was tired of her. God challenged the husband's faithfulness.

This is another thing you do: you cover the altar of the Lord with tears, with [your own] weeping and sighing, because the Lord no longer regards your offering or accepts it with favor from your hand. But you say, "Why [does He reject it]?" Because the Lord has been a witness between you and the wife of your youth, against whom you have dealt treacherously. Yet she is your marriage companion and the wife of your covenant [made by your vows]. But not one has done so who has a remnant of the Spirit. And what did that one do while seeking a godly offspring? Take heed then to your spirit, and let no one deal treacherously against the wife of your youth. "For I hate divorce," says the Lord, the God of Israel, "and him who covers his garment with wrong and violence," says the Lord of hosts. "Therefore keep watch on your spirit, so that you do not deal treacherously [with your wife]." Malachi 2:13-16 AMP

So they are no longer two, but one flesh. Therefore, what God has joined together, let no one separate. Matthew 19:6 AMP

We can make our abuser an idol.

The prohibition against adultery, not just sexual sin but failing to keep covenants, protects a marriage from breaches in trust. Both husband and wife make a vow to love, honor, and be faithful to the other. Adultery breaks trust: your spouse cannot be trusted to honor vows of faithfulness. Abuse breaks trust: your spouse cannot be trusted not to hurt you. These issues of broken trust are so great no amount of human mending or reparation can fix them. Any man who creates a breach so vast that it cannot be repaired is unfaithful in honoring the marriage covenant and is separating by his violence what God has joined together. The divorce is simply an outward sign of what has already occurred.

13. How does abuse break the marriage covenant? The abuser, _____ _____, is the one who is unfaithful and violates vows—not the person who leaves in order to be safe.

14. How can our abuser be an idol? No man can serve two masters. If we love our abuser more than we _____, there is a problem. When we are more concerned about pleasing our abuser than we are _____ _____, there is a problem. When we are more concerned about obeying our abuser than we are about _____,

there is a problem. Our first priority must always be to God. If we fill our hearts with worldly, flesh-motivated things, constantly trying to please our abuser, there is no time to please God. Instead, we can make our abuser an idol. We are seeking approval, pleasure, love, or security from our abuser instead of God.

Idols are prohibited by God. He is I AM. Whatever I need, He is. "What is an idol? It is anything more important to you than God, anything that absorbs your heart and imagination more than God, anything you seek to give you what only God can give."[4]

You shall have no other gods before Me. Exodus 20:3 NKJV

But seek ye first the kingdom of God, and his righteousness;
and all these things shall be added unto you. Matthew 6:33 KJV

Then Peter and the other apostles answered and said,
"We ought to obey God rather than men." Acts 5:29 KJV

Little children (believers, dear ones), guard yourselves from idols—[false teachings,
moral compromises, and anything that would take God's place in your heart].
1 John 5:21 AMP

15. Explain how living with an abuser can make you unstable. _____

_____

_____.

No one can serve two masters; for either he will hate the one and love the other, or he
will stand by and be devoted to the one and despise and be against the other. You cannot
serve God and mammon (deceitful riches, money, possessions, or whatever is trusted in).
Matthew 6:24 AMPC

[For being as he is] a man of two minds (hesitating, dubious, irresolute),
[he is] unstable and unreliable and uncertain about everything
[he thinks, feels, decides]. James 1:8 AMPC

Survivor: One time, I had a church commitment during a series of meetings. I was torn because I had given my word and the team was expecting me, but my abuser was demanding I stay home. I was torn between honoring my commitment to my team and honoring my commitment to my husband. I knew family comes before ministry, but I really struggled each time he would forbid me to go: my stomach would start hurting, I would cry, I would feel depressed, I would plead, I felt resentment and hurt. I felt guilt and condemnation regardless of what I did. I was so confused about what was the right thing to do. I felt I was surrendering to what I knew was a controlling spirit by obeying him. In the past, either I would stay home or he would relent and let me go.

This time felt different. Finally, I cried out to God. "God, what should I do? I don't know whether to go or stay. I don't know whether to honor my team commitments or honor my husband, even when I know he is wrong. I'm being pulled in two directions. I'm so tired of trying to figure this out. Help me, God!" God, in His infinite wisdom, gave me the perfect answer. He said, "Ask Me." What? "Just ask Me. I will tell you whether to go or whether to stay." How simple! If I asked Him and He said, "Go," I was at peace about leaving against my abuser's will. If He said stay home, I was at peace about contacting the team and telling them I couldn't be there.

This particular time, God told me to go. My abuser then gave me an ultimatum. If I left, that was it; he would not be there when I got back. He wasn't. Because I knew what God had said about going, I didn't panic or get all fearful. The next day, I arrived home after work, and my abuser was in the kitchen cooking dinner as if nothing had happened. We never spoke of it.

To live for Jesus is to throw off all the cares of this world that would hinder us from pursuing a full relationship with Jesus. We are to make as much room in our hearts for Jesus as possible. Be on guard against the tactics of our enemy who seeks to kill, steal, and destroy us and our relationship with God. Know the truth contained in His Word. Then we can combat the lies of those who weaponize Scripture for their own gain.

JOURNAL

What did you learn in this lesson? How does that knowledge change the way you think about God? How does it change the way you view your abusive relationship?

PRAYER

Holy God, I thank You for Your wisdom as revealed in Your Word. You tell me the tactics of the enemy so I can defend myself with Your truth. Forgive me, Lord, for any times that I made my abuser my idol, that I made him more important than You. Help me to be alert in the future to the enemy's lies. Let me be wise as serpents and innocent as doves. (Matthew 10:16 ESV) In the wonderful name of Jesus I pray, Amen.

Lesson 4

HOW CAN JESUS POSSIBLY UNDERSTAND MY ABUSE?

You keep track of all my sorrows. You have collected all my tears in your bottle.
You have recorded each one in your book. Psalm 56:8 NLT

Jesus was a man. How could He possibly understand my abusive situation? How can He understand my pain? A closer look at the life of Jesus indicates He experienced many of the same things as those affected by abuse. True, it was not in the context of a marriage relationship or intimate partner, but it was within the relationship of those who said they loved and wanted Him.

Complete each Scripture illustrating the abuse Jesus suffered.

1. Jesus dealt with people who wanted power and control over Him.

Then the Pharisees [argued and] said to one another, "You see that your efforts are futile.

_____

_____" John 12:19 AMP

2. He experienced the jealousy of others.

_____

_____,

and the chief priests and Pharisees sent officers to arrest him. John 7:32 ESV

3. He was insulted by others.

At this, they turned on him furiously. "You're the one who is his disciple! We are disciples of Moses. We know that God spoke to Moses, _____ _____ _____." John 9:28-29 PHILLIPS

4. He was threatened with physical abuse.

_____,

but Jesus hid himself and went out of the temple. John 8:59 ESV

_____ _____. John 10:31 AMP*

5. He was belittled (Samaritans were seen as inferior), accused of being crazy, and charged with having demons.

The Jews then said, "That clinches it. _____ _____ _____!" John 8:48 MSG

There was again a division among the Jews because of these words. _____ _____; why listen to him?" John 10:19-20 ESV

6. He was watched, followed, and provoked.

_____ *to see whether He would heal him on the Sabbath, so that they might accuse Him. Mark 3:2 MEV*

As He left there, _____ _____, and they] began to be enraged with and set themselves violently against Him and _____ _____. Luke 11:53 AMPC

7. He was falsely accused.

_____,
but their testimony did not agree. _____
_____. *Mark 14:56-57 ESV*

*Secretly watching and plotting and lying in wait for Him, _____
_____
_____. Luke 11:54 AMPC*

_____, *saying,*
"*We found this man misleading our nation and forbidding us to pay taxes to Caesar, and saying that He Himself is Christ, a King." Luke 23:2 NASB 2020*

8. He was dishonored.

*Jesus answered, "I do not have a demon, but I honor my Father, and _____
_____." John 8:49 ESV*

9. His life was threatened.

*Now when they had departed, behold, an angel of the Lord appeared to Joseph in a dream and said, "Rise, take the child and his mother, and flee to Egypt, and remain there until I tell you, for _____
_____." Matthew 2:13 ESV*

_____
_____. *Matthew 12:14 NIV*

And after these things Jesus walked in Galilee: for he would not walk in Judaea, because _____. John 7:1 ASV

"*Has not Moses given you the law? Yet none of you keeps the law. _____
_____?" John 7:19 ESV*

*It was now two days before the Passover and the Feast of Unleavened Bread. _____
_____
_____. Mark 14:1 ESV*

_____

_____. *John 11:53 ESV*

10. He was hated for telling the truth about evil.

"The world cannot hate you, _____

_____." John 7:7 ESV

11. He was arrested on false charges.

The Pharisees heard the crowd muttering these things about him, _____

_____

_____. John 7:32 ESV

12. He was physically abused.

_____

_____, and said, "Prophesy!"

_____

_____. Mark 14:65 NIV

When he said this, one of the policemen standing there _____

_____,

saying, "How dare you speak to the Chief Priest like that!" John 18:22 MSG

The men who guarded Jesus mocked Him and _____

_____. Luke 22:63 MEV

_____

_____. Matthew 27:30 NIV

But many were amazed when they saw him. _____

_____

_____. Isaiah 52:14 NLT

So then Pilate _____

_____

_____, and

put a purple robe around Him; and they kept coming up to Him, saying [mockingly],
"Hail, King of the Jews [Good health! Peace! Long life to you, King of the Jews]!" _____
_____
_____. *John 19:1-3 AMP*

13. Jesus was accused of lying when trying to defend Himself.

The Pharisees said to him, "Now you are testifying on your own behalf; _____
_____." *John 8:13 GNT*

14. He hid and escaped after being threatened.

But the Pharisees went out and plotted how they might kill Jesus. _____
_____.

A large crowd followed him, and he healed all who were ill. Matthew 12:14-15 NIV

Then they picked up stones to throw at him, _____
_____. *John 8:59 GNT*

Again they tried to seize him, _____
_____. *John 10:39 NIV*

15. He was hated.

_____
_____. *John 15:18 AMPC*

16. His friend [Lazarus] was in danger, too, because he knew the truth.

When the large crowd of the Jews learned that Jesus was there, they came, not only on
account of him but also to see Lazarus, whom he had raised from the dead. _____
_____
_____, *because*
on account of him many of the Jews were going away and believing in Jesus. John 12:9-11
ESV

17. He was betrayed by His friends.

_____ *had
given them a signal, saying, "Whomever I kiss, He is the one; seize Him and lead Him
away under guard." Mark 14:44 NASB*

*And seeing Peter warming himself, she looked at him and said, "You also were with
Jesus the Nazarene."* _____ *, saying, "I neither know nor
understand what you are talking about." And he went out onto the porch. The servant-
girl saw him, and began once more to say to the bystanders, "This is one of them!"* ___
_____ *. And after a little
while the bystanders were again saying to Peter, "Surely you are one of them, for you are
a Galilean too."* _____
_____*!" Mark 14:67-71 NASB*

18. He was denied justice.

_____
_____*. Who can speak of his descendants?
For his life was taken from the earth. Acts 8:33 NIV*

19. He was mocked.

_____
_____ *among
themselves and saying, "He saved others; He cannot save Himself." Mark 15:31 NASB*

_____
_____ *, coming up to Him, offering Him sour wine. Luke 23:36 NASB*

_____
_____ *, they stripped him of the purple cloak and
put his own clothes on him. And they led him out to crucify him. Mark 15:20 ESV*

20. He was killed.

*They nailed his hands and feet to the cross. The soldiers divided his clothing among
themselves by rolling dice to see who would win them.*_____
_____
_____*. Mark 15:24-25 TPT*

_____

_____ *they did not break His legs.*
But one of the soldiers pierced His side with a spear, and immediately blood and water came out. John 19:33-34 NKJV

Maybe you never connected your abuse with the abuse Jesus suffered at the hands of man, some by His close friends. Because of His suffering, He can understand ours. He is weeping right alongside you. Cry out to Him as you go through your healing journey. And, because He knows all things, He can give you valuable insight into your feelings and actions.

> *Because of His suffering, He can understand ours.*

> *Great is our Lord and abundant in strength;*
> *His understanding is infinite. Psalm 147:5 NASB*

Survivor: I had never thought to compare my abuse to that of Jesus. I had never recognized that He was surrounded by people who wanted power and control over Him. I had never considered that He understood my feelings of pouring my life into someone only to be mistreated and betrayed. I never connected that He also was lied to and slandered. I had never read that He was called crazy. And truly, to learn that even Jesus felt the need to hide and leave when in danger made me feel less guilty about all the times I left.

JOURNAL

What did Jesus experience that you experienced in your abusive relationship? How has this knowledge changed your view of Him?

PRAYER

My Father, I come to You as a sufferer at the hands of man. Even though Your suffering, Jesus, was so much greater than mine, You can still relate to what I have gone through and are going through now. Help me to draw closer to You as I continue on my journey of healing and wholeness. Show me the areas of my life that have been affected by my abuse that still need to be dealt with. I know You will be there helping me each and every step of the way. In Your compassionate name, Jesus, I pray, Amen.

Lesson 5

HITTING THE RESET BUTTON

For as he thinks in his heart, so is he… Proverbs 23:7 AMP

One of the things I commonly hear from survivors is that they are afraid their sons will turn out like their abuser or their daughters will end up in an abusive relationship. They may even be afraid they will again end up in another abusive relationship. We have arrived where we are because of our thinking. If we pass wrong thinking along to our children, they will pass it along to their children. Generational bondage is either something we share or something we break. Most parents want a better life for their kids than they had. The time to change wrong thinking is now, not just for our sakes but for the sake of our future generations.

As we were growing up, the enemy established strongholds in our thinking.

• We may have been told we were fat, stupid, or lazy.

• We may have been told we weren't as talented, pretty, or smart as others.

• We may have been told we weren't wanted, we ruined a parent's life, or we weren't loved.

• We may have been told we weren't loveable, desirable, or worthy.

• We may have been told we would never amount to anything, would never have a decent job, or could never attract a good man.

- We may have been told we'd never change, we'll end up just like so-and-so, or we're the problem.

Even now, as adults, those same patterns of thinking can be affecting our lives.

- We may be filled with feelings of inadequacy and inferiority.

- We may be insecure about our appearance.

- We may feel inadequate due to our lack of education or training.

- We may suffer with feelings of abandonment, rejection, or both.

- We may be bound by prejudices and stereotypes.

Lean on, trust in, and be confident in the Lord with all your heart and mind and do not rely on your own insight or understanding. Proverbs 3:5 AMPC

For in Christ Jesus you are all sons of God, through faith. For as many of you as were baptized into Christ have put on Christ. There is neither Jew nor Greek, there is neither slave nor free, there is no male and female, for you are all one in Christ Jesus. Galatians 3:26-28 ESV

PATTERNS OF THINKING

Our way of thinking comes from our family, our experiences, our personality, our decisions, and what we have learned from others.[5] Our thinking affects our response to hard times, conflicts, opportunities, and victories. God wants us to experience freedom from wrong thinking and experience His joy on our life's journey now, not just in eternity.

"For I know the plans and thoughts that I have for you," says the Lord, "plans for peace and well-being and not for disaster, to give you a future and a hope." Jeremiah 29:11 AMP

The Lord makes firm the steps of the one who delights in him; though he may stumble, he will not fall, for the Lord upholds him with his hand. Psalm 37:23-24 NIV

We have a choice of how we respond to difficulties and conflict. I'm not talking about times with our abuser where the conflict is dangerous or life-threatening. I'm talking about the day-to-day conflicts with family, friends, co-workers, neighbors, and even strangers. In the past, when you have been confronted with stressful hard times and challenges, which unhealthy ways of coping have you used?

- Walking or running away

- Getting angry or fighting back

- Muttering and complaining

- Excusing, justifying, or rationalizing

- Assuming or accepting blame

- Blaming others

- Overeating or failing to eat

- Hurting yourself or others

- Ignoring the situation and letting whatever happens happen

- Sleeping or avoiding

- Other _____

Instead of talking to God about our problems, we should talk to our problems about God.

One of the most profound sermons I ever heard was based on Mark 11:23 (AMP):

I assure you and most solemnly say to you, whoever says to this mountain, "Be lifted up and thrown into the sea!" and does not doubt in his heart [in God's unlimited power], but believes that what he says is going to take place, it will be done for him [in accordance with God's will].

Instead of talking to God about our problems, we should talk to our problems about God. We need to find an answer to our problem in His Word and declare His Word to the problem.

1. Instead of telling God about your bank account balance, tell your bank account balance _____

_____

_____. *Philippians 4:19 ESV*

2. Instead of telling God about the accusing words of others, speak aloud _____

_____

_____. *Romans 8:1 ESV*

3. Instead of looking disparagingly in the mirror at your reflection, tell your reflection

_____

_____

_____

_____. *Psalm 139:14 AMP*

4. Instead of telling God you are not smart enough, say aloud _____

_____

_____. *Ecclesiastes 2:26 ESV*

5. Instead of telling God you can't handle all this stress, tell your stress _____

_____

_____

_____. *Isaiah 26:3 NKJV*

6. Instead of telling God about all the needs in your life, tell your needs _____

_____

_____

_____. *Matthew 6:33 NKJV*

7. Instead of telling God about how everything is going wrong, say aloud _____

_____

_____

_____

_____

_____

_____. *Psalm 91:14-15 NKJV*

Hard times will come. However, the way we approach those hard times makes all the difference. Changing our thinking is the first step.

In the past, when we have been confronted with opportunities, our way of coping may have been one of these:

- Being paralyzed by indecision and over-analysis

- Being overcome with fear of failure

- Avoidance

- Feeling unworthy or undeserving

- Expecting something bad will happen

In the past when we have been confronted with victories, our way of coping may have been one of these:

- Minimizing our success

- Fearing future failure

- Feeling unworthy or undeserving

- Expecting something bad will happen

Once again, instead of speaking your old thoughts, speak your new thoughts—the Word of God—to combat the old way of thinking.

I believe God is a good God who wants His best for me. I believe He has a plan for my life. I may not understand what is happening, but I believe whatever happens, He will turn it to good.

1. Instead of thinking you don't know what to do, say _____. *Psalm 121:1-2 ESV*

2. Instead of thinking you might fail, say _____." *2 Corinthians 12:9 ESV*

3. Instead of thinking you don't deserve success, say _____. *Deuteronomy 8:18 ESV*

4. Instead of thinking something bad might happen, say _____. *Philippians 4:8 ESV*

WHY IT'S HARD TO CHANGE THE WAY WE THINK

Our thinking patterns are usually firmly entrenched. When someone challenges our thinking, our first response is to get defensive, dig our heels in, and hold even more tightly to what we believe.[6] Our biggest stumbling block to changing how we think is ourselves. Few people enjoy being told they are wrong. Change requires work. Our attitude may be one of these:

- I am comfortable with my way of thinking.

- It's the only thinking I know.

- I think my thoughts are right.

- I think my thoughts make sense.

It's time to run our thoughts through the filter of God's Word.

Let me ask you, then, "How's that way of thinking working for you? Do you have the relationships with your spouse, children, and extended family you want? Do you have the friends you want? Do you have the relationship with God you want?" If you answered, "No," to any of these questions, you can choose to think differently.

It's time to bring every thought captive. It's time to run our thoughts through the filter of God's Word. It's time to put off our old way of thinking and put on a new way of thinking. When we are battling against thinking patterns developed over a long time period, we cannot battle alone. We need God's help. When we lean on our own understanding based on our experiences, we are not trusting in His truth.

Jesus came to set us free from the bondage of the enemy. Our enemy comes to kill, steal, and destroy. Our Savior comes to give us a full, superabundant, satisfying, superior life. When we hold onto the very things that keep us from experiencing the life He designed for us, for which He died for us, we are insulting God. We are saying, "Jesus dying was not enough." Ouch!

Nevertheless, let it be according to Your Word.

We must align our thinking with His Word. We need a "nevertheless moment."

Survivor: I was complaining to a family member about a problem I had that didn't seem to be getting any better. He reminded me of the story of Jesus telling Peter to throw his nets on the other side of the boat, and Peter argued back that they had been fishing all night with no success. I think Peter suddenly realized with whom he was speaking: Jesus who fed the 5,000, Jesus who paid taxes with a gold coin from a fish's mouth, Jesus who healed the sick, Jesus who cast out demons, Jesus who rose from the dead. Peter had a "nevertheless moment." He said, "Nevertheless, at your Word I will let down the net." He went on to catch so many fish the net began breaking. When I am talking about my circumstances and am speaking against what God says, I need a "nevertheless moment." Now, when I catch myself speaking against what the Scriptures say, I quickly add, "But nevertheless, let it be according to Your Word."

When you suffer from feelings of abandonment or rejection, speak the Word of God. When you are paralyzed by indecision and over-analysis, speak the Word of God. When you are battling with a fear of failure, speak the Word of God. When you feel as if you want to avoid facing something, speak the Word of God. When you experience feelings of inadequacy and inferiority, speak the Word of God. When you can't seem to shake that black cloud hovering over you, speak the Word of God. It's not about what you have learned from your family, your studies, your friends, or even your experiences; it's about what God says. It's not about your wrong thinking; it's about God's right thinking.

TEARING DOWN STRONGHOLDS AND CASTING DOWN IMAGINATIONS

When we have years and years of responding negatively to life's events and circumstances, we make ourselves vulnerable to sickness and diseases. Our brains are designed to hear and obey God. When we listen to the Holy Spirit, we have the mighty power of God moving through our minds that positively affects our brains. It is through the conscious mind that we make changes to our thinking.[7]

Strongholds are those areas in our lives that we have had difficulty overcoming. Because we are fighting a spiritual battle, we cannot use natural weapons such as willpower, determination, or worldly techniques. We must use spiritual weapons that are divinely empowered to destroy—not just knock down—strongholds and gain control of our thoughts, so they line up with what the Word of God says.

For though we walk in the flesh, we are not waging war according to the flesh. For the weapons of our warfare are not of the flesh but have divine power to destroy strongholds. We destroy arguments and every lofty opinion raised against the knowledge of God, and take every thought captive to obey Christ, being ready to punish every disobedience, when your obedience is complete. 2 Corinthians 10:3-6 ESV

Survivor: I used to slip into the bathroom and recite Scriptures in a whisper when I could sense he was escalating. It helped me stay calm and clear-headed so I could better discern if we needed to escape.

How do we get rid of our old ways of thinking, these strongholds which are so displeasing to God, when they've been a part of us for so long? Start with the following steps.

1. _____ to help us identify our wrong way of thinking.

> *If any of you lacks wisdom, let him ask God, who gives generously*
> *to all without reproach, and it will be given him. James 1:5 ESV*

Keep in mind that the enemy's tactic is to condemn you with generalities.

- I am awful. I have horrendous strongholds. I'm ashamed and unworthy of God's love.

- I am such a loser. Nobody likes me. I'll never amount to anything.

- Everybody else is getting blessed. I'm doing something wrong again.

God's way of correcting us is to convict us with specifics.

- Speak to your children in love, not anger.

- I created you to be a servant leader, not a demanding boss.

- Your fear of lack is hindering the destiny I have for you.

Generalities immobilize while specifics motivate.[8]

2. _____ and _____ for thinking contrary to God's Word.

> *If we confess our sins, he is faithful and just and will forgive us our sins*
> *and purify us from all unrighteousness. 1 John 1:9 NIV*

> *He who covers his sins will not prosper, but whoever confesses*
> *and forsakes them will have mercy. Proverbs 28:13 NKJV*

> *Repent therefore and be converted, that your sins may be blotted out, so that times of*
> *refreshing may come from the presence of the Lord. Acts 3:19 NKJV*

3. _____ arguments and opinions that are contrary to God's Word. Use divinely powerful spiritual weapons to fight a spiritual war.

For the weapons of our warfare are not of the flesh but have divine power to destroy strongholds. We destroy arguments and every lofty opinion raised against the knowledge of God, and take every thought captive to obey Christ. 2 Corinthians 10:4-5 ESV

And take the helmet of salvation, and the sword of the Spirit,
which is the word of God. Ephesians 6:17 ESV

4. _____ and be transformed into His image. Choose to think differently; want to think differently. Nothing changes until our thoughts change.

Have this mind among yourselves, which is yours in Christ Jesus. Philippians 2:5 ESV

For as he thinks within himself, so he is. Proverbs 23:7 NASB

And do not be conformed to this world, but be transformed by the renewing of your mind, that you may prove what is that good and acceptable and perfect will of God.
Romans 12:2 NKJV

But we all, with unveiled face, beholding as in a mirror the glory of the Lord,
are being transformed into the same image from glory to glory,
just as by the Spirit of the Lord. 2 Corinthians 3:18 NKJV

5. _____ based on new thinking that demonstrates and reinforces the desire to change your thinking. Set your mind on things above—His ways. Let go of old arguments, old opinions, old patterns, and old ways of thinking that you previously accepted. Run your thoughts through a Scripture filter to make sure they line up with what God says. Let your actions align with your new way of thinking. You can do it!

Destroy arguments and opinions that are contrary to God's Word.

But prove yourselves doers of the word [actively and continually obeying God's precepts], and not merely listeners [who hear the word but fail to internalize its meaning], deluding yourselves [by unsound reasoning contrary to the truth]. James 1:22 AMP

And set your minds and keep them set on what is above (the higher things), not on the things that are on the earth. Colossians 3:2 AMPC

And I am sure of this, that He who began a good work in you will bring it to completion at the day of Jesus Christ. Philippians 1:6 ESV

I can do all things through Him who strengthens me. Philippians 4:14 ESV

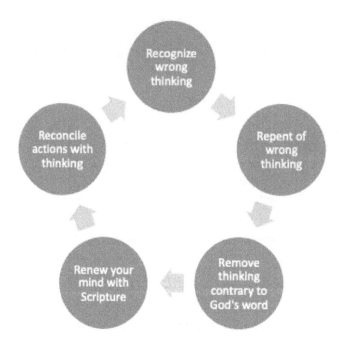

Changing our thinking is an ongoing journey. Old thoughts we didn't recognize before as needing to be destroyed will surface. New thoughts might begin to take root before we remember to filter them through God's Word. Being around certain people or in certain circumstances may cause us to revert to old ways of thinking. Use the diagram to help you in your journey to hitting the reset button.

As Christians, we should make it our goal to avoid thinking or confessing any of the things that are against God's Word.

> **Survivor**: As a teacher, I was always conscious of the words I used with my students. When I noticed my students' behavior deteriorating, I would check the amount of negativity I was speaking. I used pennies to keep track of how many times I spoke negatively instead of positively to them. It never failed that as my language became more positive, the more I enjoyed my job and the better their behavior became. By just being aware of my word choices and choosing to speak differently, I affected my own attitude along with the attitude and behavior of the people around me. The same technique works for monitoring the number of times we speak words that are contrary to God's Word. Try it.

Death and life are in the power of the tongue, And those
who love it will eat its fruit. Proverbs 18:21 NKJV

For by your words you will be justified, and by your words
you will be condemned. Matthew 12:37 NKJV

To help him overcome his habit of negative speaking, Don Gossett wrote a "My Never Again List" in his book, *What You Say is What You Get*. He took the liberty of personalizing some of these King James Version Scriptures as indicated in brackets.

MY NEVER AGAIN LIST[9]

Never again will I confess *"I can't,"* for **I can do all things through Christ which strengtheneth me. Philippians 4:13**

Never again will I confess lack, for **my God shall supply all of [my] needs according to his riches in glory by Christ Jesus. Philippians 4:19**

Never again will I confess fear, for **God hath not given [me] the spirit of fear, but of power, and of love, and of a sound mind. 2 Timothy 1:7**

Never again will I confess doubt and lack of faith, for **God hath dealt to every man the measure of faith. Romans 12:3**

Never again will I confess weakness, for **the Lord is the strength of my life. Psalm 27:1** and **The people that know their God shall be strong and do exploits. Daniel 11:32**

Never again will I confess supremacy of Satan over my life, for *greater is he that is in [me] than he that is in the world. 1 John 4:4*

Never again will I confess defeat, for *God always causeth [me] to triumph in Christ. 2 Corinthians 2:14*

Never again will I confess lack of wisdom, for *Christ Jesus who of God is made unto [me] wisdom. 1 Corinthians 1:30*

Never again will I confess sickness, for *with his stripes [I am] healed. Isaiah 53:5* and Jesus *Himself took [my] infirmities and bare [my] sicknesses. Matthew 8:17*

Never again will I confess worries and frustrations, for I am *casting all [my] cares upon him who careth for [me]. 1 Peter 5:7*

Never again will I confess bondage, for *where the Spirit of the Lord is, there is liberty. 2 Corinthians 3:17*

Never again will I confess condemnation, for *there is therefore now no condemnation to them which are in Christ Jesus. Romans 8:1*

Following Gosset's pattern using the King James Version, I added the following Never Again confessions:

Never again will I confess I am unlovable, for *beloved, now are we the sons of God. 1 John 3:2* and *I have loved you with an everlasting love. Jeremiah 31:3*

Never again will I confess loneliness, for Jesus said, "*Lo, I am with you always, even unto the end of the world." Matthew 28:20* and *I will never leave thee, nor forsake thee. Hebrews 13:5*

Never again will I confess discontentment, for *I have learned, in whatsoever state [circumstances] I am, therewith to be content. Philippians 4:11*

Never again will I confess unworthiness, for *he hath made him to be sin for us, who knew no sin, that we might be made the righteousness of God in him. 2 Corinthians 5:21*

Never again will I confess confusion, for *God is not the author of confusion, but of peace. 1 Corinthians 14:33*

Never again will I confess persecution, for *if God be for us, who can be against us? Romans 8:31*

Never again will I confess the dominion of sin over my life, for *the Law of the Spirit of life in Christ Jesus hath made me free from the law of sin and death. Romans 8:2* and *As far as the east is from the west, so far hath he removed our transgressions from us. Psalm 103:12*

Never again will I confess insecurity, for *when thou liest down, thou shalt not be afraid; yea, thou shalt lie down, and thy sleep shall be sweet ... for the Lord shall be thy confidence, and shall keep thy foot from being taken. Proverbs 3:24, 26*

Never again will I confess failure, for *nay, in all these things we are more than conquerors through him that loves us. Romans 8:37*

Never again will I confess frustration, for *thou wilt keep him in perfect peace, whose mind is stayed on thee: because he trusteth in thee. Isaiah 26:3*

Never again will I confess fear of the future, for *as it is written, eye hath not seen, nor ear heard, neither hath entered into the heart of man, the things which God hath prepared for them that love him. 1 Corinthians 2:9*

Never again will I confess troubles, for Jesus said, *"In the world ye shall have tribulation: but be of good cheer; I have overcome the world." John 16:33*

Never again will I confess I'm unacceptable, for *he has made us accepted in the beloved. Ephesians 1:6*

> *We should make it our goal to avoid thinking or confessing any of the things that are against God's Word.*

As our faith builds, we may be tempted to say these Scriptures boldly aloud in the presence of our abuser. While I am a strong advocate for speaking God's word aloud, it is inadvisable and can be dangerous to speak aloud these Scriptures directly to your abuser, especially when he is escalating, unless you are absolutely certain the Holy Spirit is leading you. Declaring Scriptures aloud in your home when he is not there is much safer. You are still building yourself up in the Word and releasing the power of the Word. Be aware that darkness does not like light and may want to prevent you from releasing His word.

The Light shines on in the darkness, and the darkness did not understand it or overpower it or appropriate it or absorb it [and is unreceptive to it]. John 1:5 AMP

JOURNAL

In what areas did God reveal your wrong way of thinking? What else did God show you in this lesson?

PRAYER

Almighty God, I am so thankful that You have given me a sound mind to change my way of thinking if I choose. You have given me mighty weapons to pull down the strongholds in my mind, so I am not passing on unhealthy thinking to future generations. I thank You for Your Word that I can use as a sword to defeat the attacks of the enemy on my mind. Help me, Father, by showing me the areas of my thinking that are not yet conformed to Your way of thinking. I repent now for every time I have spoken words that are not in agreement with Your Word. I commit to making my actions line up with my new way of thinking. I know this is an ongoing process, but I choose to start today. In the powerful name of Jesus I pray, Amen.

Lesson 6

HEALING TRUTHS

If you are tired from carrying heavy burdens, come to me and
I will give you rest. Take the yoke I give you. Put it on your shoulders
and learn from me. I am gentle and humble, and you will find rest.
This yoke is easy to bear, and this burden is light. Matthew 11:28-30 CEV

Living in an abusive situation is frightening. You never know from when and where the next attack will come. You constantly walk around as if walking on eggshells. You are hypervigilant to every word, sound, tone, and action.

Survivor: I still don't like the sound of tires crunching on gravel. That sound when I was with my abuser indicated he was home. The knots would begin in my stomach. I frantically tried to recall if there was any reason for him to be mad. All my senses went on high alert. I quickly checked to make sure that anything or anyone who might trigger his anger was not in his line of sight. I could tell from how he shut the truck door, how he walked across the porch, how he opened and shut the front door, how he looked at me when he walked in, even the color of his eyes, before he ever said a word, what kind of night it was going to be. It was exhausting.

Just as glass breaks when it is under stress, you may have parts of you that are as broken as shattered glass. Just because something is broken, doesn't mean it isn't beautiful. There is an art form called Kintsugi, the art of using liquid metal, often gold, to repair broken pottery. Instead of being cast aside as useless, the broken pottery is repaired. The breakage is considered part of the history of the pottery rather than something to be disguised. All things, including our broken pieces, can be transformed by the right hands. Although stained glass doesn't use broken pieces, it still represents the beauty that comes when individual pieces are artfully crafted to fit together. Picture yourself as beautiful pieces of stained glass just waiting to be arranged by the Master. Get a vision for how your glass masterpiece will look when all the pieces are placed in the perfect spot.

For we are God's masterpiece. He has created us anew in Christ Jesus,
so we can do the good things he planned for us long ago. Ephesians 2:10 NLT

No matter what anyone says, no matter our circumstances, we will stand and not be moved with lies.

What about the pieces that don't seem to fit? Some pieces were never meant to be there. Those are the lies of the enemy that keep your pieces from ever forming the masterpiece they are intended to be. With the leading of the Holy Spirit, you can separate the truth pieces from the lie pieces.

Going through abuse can shake our faith. Our abuser's lies can often become our truth. What we must develop is unshakeable faith that comes from knowing God, His Word, His character, and His nature. Then, no matter what anyone says, no matter our circumstances, we will stand and not be moved with lies. We will remain firmly rooted and grounded in His truth. We will be as immovable as stone.

He is like a tree planted by water, that sends out its roots by the stream,
and does not fear when heat comes, for its leaves remain green, and is not
anxious in the year of drought, for it does not cease to bear fruit. Jeremiah 17:8 ESV

Therefore whoever hears these sayings of Mine, and does them, I will liken him to a wise
man who built his house on the rock: and the rain descended, the floods came, and the
winds blew and beat on that house; and it did not fall, for it was founded on the rock.
Matthew 7:24-25 NKJV

But the Lord GOD helps me; therefore I have not been disgraced; therefore I have set my face like a flint, and I know that I shall not be put to shame. Isaiah 50:7 ESV

Survivor: My abuser was a name-caller, as are most of them. He would call me the most awful names that I won't repeat. I knew I was faithful so accusations of sleeping with someone else didn't change how I felt about myself. After we separated, his family accused me of being a hypocrite and not a real Christian. As hurtful as those accusations were, I knew they weren't true. It didn't change who God said I was. When one of my own family members falsely accused me of something my abuser said I had done, it hurt, but it didn't change the truth: I didn't do what I was accused of doing. None of these people were able to convince me that I was who they said I was. Knowing the truth about who I am makes it easier not to take offense when others have a different opinion of me. I can't change what they think. I rest in the knowledge that God knows the truth.

Knowing the truth about who I am makes it easier not to take offense when others have a different opinion of me.

Reading and meditating on His Word helps us re-establish foundational truths that cannot be shaken regardless of the circumstances in your life. These are the truths we hold onto when our abuser is saying exactly the opposite. When he speaks death, God speaks life. When he speaks hatred, God speaks love. When he speaks violence, God speaks peace. When he speaks hurt, God speaks healing. Let's look at some truths about God.

TRUTH 1: GOD IS GOOD.

Regardless of your circumstances, what you feel, or what you think, God is _____ all the time, and everything He does is _____.

You are good, and do good; Teach me Your statutes. Psalm 119:68 NKJV

Oh, give thanks to the LORD, for He is good!
For His mercy endures forever. Psalm 136:1 NKJV

Praise the Lord! Oh give thanks to the Lord, for He is good;
for His lovingkindness is everlasting. Psalm 106:1 NASB

Praise the Lord, for the Lord is good; sing praises to his name,
for that is pleasant. Psalm 135:3 NIV

TRUTH 2: GOD LOVES YOU.

The reason God _____ you has nothing to do with you and everything to do with who He is. God _____ you before you _____ Him. His _____ cannot be earned. It was bought with the blood on the cross; paid for in full. It is unconditional _____ so there is nothing you can do to make Him _____ you more or less. Whether you choose to _____ God or not, He still _____ you. He will _____ you even if you refuse to accept His _____, but you will not receive the benefits of His intimate _____ that comes from being in a personal relationship with Him. God _____ you because God is _____. It is hard to comprehend such an unconditional _____, but if you can believe it and receive it, His _____ will transform your life.

But God demonstrates his own love for us in this:
While we were still sinners, Christ died for us. Romans 5:8 NIV

Behold what manner of love the Father has bestowed on us, that we should be called
children of God! Therefore the world does not know us, because it did not know Him.
Beloved, now we are children of God; and it has not yet been revealed what we shall be,
but we know that when He is revealed, we shall be like Him,
for we shall see Him as He is. 1 John 3:1-2 NKJV

For God so loved the world, that he gave his only Son, that whoever
believes in him should not perish but have eternal life. John 3:16 ESV

neither the world above nor the world below—there is nothing in all
creation that will ever be able to separate us from the love of God
which is ours through Christ Jesus our Lord. Romans 8:39 GNT

The earth is filled with your love, Lord.... Psalm 119:64 NIV

We love because he first loved us. 1 John 4:19 ESV

"Though the mountains be shaken and the hills be removed,
yet my unfailing love for you will not be shaken
nor my covenant of peace be removed," says the Lord,
who has compassion on you. Isaiah 54:10 NIV

TRUTH 3: GOD'S PLANS FOR US GIVE US A HOPE, A FUTURE, AND A FULL LIFE. HE WORKS FOR OUR GOOD.

Sometimes you may feel as if living one more day is too hard. You have lost all _____. The enemy would love nothing more than for you to give up, but God wants you to choose to have a _____. Every survivor that has come before you wants you to keep going. One day at a time, you move toward your _____. God longs for us to experience all the joy He designed for us to know. We only find true and lasting joy and fulfillment in Him. He alone satisfies. He alone works for our _____. He alone gives _____ and perfect gifts.

"For I know the plans I have for you," declares the LORD, "plans to prosper you and not
to harm you, plans to give you hope and a future." Jeremiah 29:11NIV

The thief comes only to steal and kill and destroy; I have come
that they may have life, and have it to the full. John 10:10 NIV

We know that God is always at work for the good of everyone who loves him. They are
the ones God has chosen for his purpose, and he has always known who his chosen ones
would be. He had decided to let them become like his own Son, so that his Son would be
the first of many children. Romans 8:28-29 CEV

Every good thing given and every perfect gift is from above, coming down from the
Father of lights, with whom there is no variation or shifting shadow. James 1:17 NASB

*If you then, being evil, know how to give good gifts to your children,
how much more will your Father who is in heaven give
what is good to those who ask Him! Matthew 7:11 NASB*

*For I am confident of this very thing, that He who began a good work
in you will perfect it until the day of Christ Jesus. Philippians 1:6 NASB*

TRUTH 4: WE ARE CHOSEN BY GOD BECAUSE OF OUR RELATIONSHIP WITH CHRIST.

The words and actions of the people around us can be hurtful. We may feel rejected and unworthy. But if we are in Christ, we are _____ by God. In other words, once we belong to God through receiving Christ, there is nothing we can do or say that will make us *more* _____. God _____ us because He wanted us as His. Because Jesus is acceptable to God and we have a relationship with Jesus, we are acceptable to God.

*Just as [in His love] He chose us in Christ [actually selected us for Himself as His own]
before the foundation of the world, so that we would be holy [that is, consecrated, set
apart for Him, purpose-driven] and blameless in His sight. In love He predestined and
lovingly planned for us to be adopted to Himself as [His own] children through Jesus
Christ, in accordance with the kind intention and good pleasure of His will—to the
praise of His glorious grace and favor, which He so freely bestowed on us in the Beloved
[His Son, Jesus Christ]. Ephesians 1:4-6 AMP*

TRUTH 5: GOD SUPPLIES FOR OUR EVERY NEED. HIS GRACE IS SUFFICIENT.

No matter what we _____, God is enough. When all we have is gone, He hasn't even begun to tap into His endless supply of resources. When we are weak, He is _____. When we are tired, He is our _____. When we face the impossible, He makes all things _____. When we are troubled, He is _____. When we are sick, He is _____. When we are brokenhearted, He binds our _____. We can learn to lean wholly on God. Whatever we're going through, God's _____ is there in abundant supply. He never runs out of _____. His _____ is sufficient to

deal with our past experiences, mistakes, hurts, and failures. His _____
is sufficient for the most scarred, broken, and traumatized among us.

Because the Lord is my Shepherd, I have everything I need! Psalm 23:1 TLB

*And my God will supply every need of yours according
to his riches in glory in Christ Jesus. Philippians 4:19 ESV*

*Therefore do not be anxious, saying, "What shall we eat?" or "What shall we drink?"
or "What shall we wear?" For the Gentiles seek after all these things, and your heavenly
Father knows that you need them all. Matthew 6:31-32 ESV*

*But he said to me, "My grace is sufficient for you, for my power is made perfect in
weakness." Therefore I will boast all the more gladly of my weaknesses, so that the power
of Christ may rest upon me. 2 Corinthians 12:9 ESV*

I can do all things through him who strengthens me. Philippians 4:13 ESV

*Even young people get tired, then stumble and fall. But those who trust the Lord will find
new strength. They will be strong like eagles soaring upward on wing;, they will walk and
run without getting tired. Isaiah 40:30-31 CEV*

But he said, "What is impossible with men is possible with God." Luke 18:27 ESV

*Peace I leave with you, My peace I give to you; not as the world gives do I give to you. Let
not your hearts be troubled, neither let it be afraid. John 14:27 NKJV*

*Bless the Lord, my soul, and do not forget any of His benefits; Who pardons all your
guilt, Who heals all your diseases. Psalm 103:2-3 NASB*

*He heals the brokenhearted and binds up their wounds [healing their pain and
comforting their sorrow]. Psalm 147:3 AMP*

And God is able to make all grace abound to you, so that having all sufficiency in all things at all times, you may abound in every good work. 2 Corinthians 9:8 ESV

TRUTH 6: JESUS IS OUR PROTECTOR.

Jesus is our safe place and our hope. He comes to _____ us from abusive pain and oppressors. He _____ us day and night; He never sleeps.

Those who go to God Most High for safety will be protected by the Almighty. I will say to the Lord, "You are my place of safety and protection. You are my God and I trust you."
Psalm 91:1-2 NCV

You are my hiding place! You protect me from trouble, and you put songs in my heart because you have saved me. Psalm 32:7 CEV

You, Lord God, are my protector. Rescue me and keep me safe from all who chase me. Or else they will rip me apart like lions attacking a victim, and no one will save me. I am innocent, Lord God! Psalm 7:1-3 CEV

I look to the hills! Where will I find help? It will come from the Lord, who created the heavens and the earth. The Lord is your protector, and he won't go to sleep or let you stumble. The protector of Israel doesn't doze or ever get drowsy. The Lord is your protector, there at your right side to shade you from the sun. You won't be harmed by the sun during the day or by the moon at night. The Lord will protect you and keep you safe from all dangers. The Lord will protect you now and always wherever you go.
Psalm 121:1-8 CEV

You listen to the longings of those who suffer. You offer them hope, and you pay attention to their cries for help. You defend orphans and everyone else in need, so that no one on earth can terrify others again.
Psalm 10:17-18 CEV

Domestic violence is not a result of God's punishment because of something we have done.

TRUTH 7: JESUS WAS SENT BY GOD TO OFFER FREEDOM TO ANYONE WHO SUFFERS.

Domestic violence is not a result of God's punishment because of something we have done. Abuse is the result of the abuser's sin. The responsibility for your _____ lies at the hands of the abuser. Being in an abusive relationship can feel as if you are in a prison. God provides a way to _____ _____ to all who are oppressed and _____.

Love the Lord and hate evil! God protects his loyal people
and rescues them from violence. Psalm 97:10 CEV

Jesus went back to Nazareth, where he had been brought up, and as usual he went to the meeting place on the Sabbath. When he stood up to read from the Scriptures, he was given the book of Isaiah the prophet. He opened it and read, "The Lord's Spirit has come to me, because he has chosen me to tell the good news to the poor. The Lord has sent me to announce freedom for prisoners, to give sight to the blind, to free everyone who suffers, and to say, 'This is the year the Lord has chosen.'" Jesus closed the book, then handed it back to the man in charge and sat down. Everyone in the meeting place looked straight at Jesus. Then Jesus said to them, "What you have just heard me read has come true today." Luke 4:16-21 CEV

TRUTH 8: GOD IS ALWAYS WITH YOU, HOLDING YOUR HAND, AND GUIDING YOU.

You may not always feel God's presence or see Him at work in your life. Nevertheless, God's Word assures you that He is _____, close enough to hold your _____. He will _____ you through your hard times.

Don't be afraid. I am with you. Don't tremble with fear. I am your God. I will make you strong, as I protect you with my arm and give you victories. I am the Lord your God. I am holding your hand, so don't be afraid. I am here to help you. Isaiah 41:10, 13 CEV

Be strong. Take courage. Don't be intimidated. Don't give them a second thought because God, your God, is striding ahead of you. He's right there with you. He won't let you down; he won't leave you. Deuteronomy 31:6 MSG

Nevertheless, I am continually with You; You hold me by my right hand. Psalm 73:23 NKJV

However, when He, the Spirit of truth, has come, He will guide you into all truth; for He will not speak on His own authority, but whatever He hears He will speak; and He will tell you things to come. John 16:13 NKJV

The steps of a good man are ordered by the LORD, And He delights in his way. Psalm 37:23 NKJV

TRUTH 9: THE LORD BRINGS JUSTICE.

Many of you have personal experience that real-life court proceedings and outcomes can be very different from those portrayed on TV. You may have experienced injustice in man's court, but God assures us His _____ will prevail. And whose _____ would you prefer to have: man's or God's?

For all who are mistreated, the Lord brings justice. Psalm 103:6 CEV

God judges by what is right, and God is always ready to punish the wicked. Psalm 7:11 NCV

Your love, O Lord, reaches to the heavens, your faithfulness to the skies. Your righteousness is like the mighty mountains, your justice like the great deep. You, Lord, preserve both people and animals. Psalm 36:5-6 NIV

You keep track of all my sorrows. You have collected all my tears in your bottle. You have recorded each one in your book. Psalm 56:8 NLT

TRUTH 10: THE LORD UNDERSTANDS THE EFFECTS OF ABUSE. HE WANTS YOU TO BE MADE WHOLE.

The Lord is omniscient—He knows everything your abuser has done to you and your family. He sees the brokenness caused by the effects of abuse. However, He is the master fixer-upper. He created you with three parts: body, soul (mind, will, and emotions), and spirit. He wants you physically _____, emotionally _____, and spiritually _____. He knows how to take your brokenness and make *all* of you _____. You will know you are on the road to _____ when you start to see the effects of _____ on your life. The Bible calls these effects the fruit of the spirit: _____, _____, _____, _____, _____, _____, _____, _____, and _____.

May God himself, the God who makes everything holy and whole, make you holy and whole, put you together—spirit, soul, and body—and keep you fit for the coming of our Master, Jesus Christ. 1 Thessalonians 5:23 MSG

Therefore, if anyone is in Christ, he is a new creation; old things have passed away; behold, all things have become new. 2 Corinthians 5:17 NKJV

But the fruit of the Spirit is love, joy, peace, patience, kindness, goodness, faithfulness, gentleness, self-control; against such things there is no law. Galatians 5:22-23 ESV

JOURNAL

Write down your favorites of God's truths. Explain how these truths help you on your journey to becoming "not that woman anymore." What changes do you see in your life already?

PRAYER

Blessed Father, I am so grateful for who You are. I am overwhelmed by Your goodness and faithfulness. You have shown me in Your Word the truths that I need to know so my soul will prosper. Help me embrace each truth and make it part of me. Show me, Father, the work You are doing in my life. I trust that whatever You are doing for me, in me, and through me as a result of my brokenness is for my good and will bring You glory. Help me see my brokenness in light of Your great design for my life. Help me move from broken pieces to masterpiece. Help me show evidence of good spiritual fruit. I love You, Father. In the beautiful name of Jesus I pray, Amen.

Healing Truths Activity

FAUX STAINED GLASS*

Below is an overview of the project. For a full list of materials and step-by-step instructions, check out the links below.

https://suzyssitcom.com/2011/01/feature-friday-faux-stained-glass.html/2

https://www.youtube.com/watch?v=FxR3FzXzRcY

https://www.youtube.com/watch?v=f6HQIIqgtkI

This project involves using a simple pattern, perhaps from a coloring book or printed from an online source, taped to the underside of a piece of glass, plastic, or plexiglass removed from a picture frame. The pattern is then traced onto the glass, plastic, or plexiglass with a thin marker. (Some videos skip this step.) Using quality white glue mixed with a bit of black acrylic paint to simulate the look of lead, trace over the pattern lines on the glass. When the black outline has dried, paint to fill in the outlines using separate containers of clear quality glue mixed with a small amount of selected acrylic paint colors. Let dry.

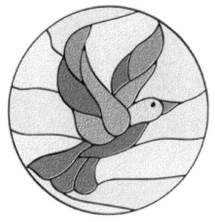

Place the completed faux stained glass back into the picture frame. The resulting faux stain glass serves as a reminder that our pieces can also fit together to create something beautiful.

This activity will take more than one session to allow for drying time.

Lesson 7

GOD OUR HEALER

He heals the brokenhearted and binds up their wounds [healing their pain and comforting their sorrow]. Psalm 147:3 AMP

As Christians, we believe that all healing comes from God. Once we gain that revelation, all the trials, tragedies, traumas, and turmoil of earthly living can be turned over to Him. He *is* Jehovah Rophe. He is Healer. YHWH-Rophe (pronounced Yä-wá´ Roh-fee´) is the second name God used to reveal Himself to His people.

So he cried out to the Lord, and the Lord showed him a tree. When he cast it into the waters, the waters were made sweet. There He made a statute and an ordinance for them, and there He tested them, and said, "If you diligently heed the voice of the Lord your God and do what is right in His sight, give ear to His commandments and keep all His statutes, I will put none of the diseases on you which I have brought on the Egyptians. For I am the Lord who heals you." Exodus 15:25-26 NKJV

As an advocate for women who have suffered intimate partner abuse, I'm heartbroken to hear week after week the vile experiences of women who are called fearfully and wonderfully made by our Heavenly Father. They are degraded and humiliated by the very person who has been entrusted to represent the love of the Father for His bride.

The scars begin to form with each hurtful word, accusation, threat, and act of violence against those in abusive situations. Just as a paper folded multiple times cannot be easily smoothed out to its original condition, so our wounded bodies, souls, and spirits cannot be easily smoothed back to pre-abuse condition by earthly methods. So many survivors of domestic violence already had scars and wounds way before entering their abusive relationship.

God wants to do something no doctor or counselor can do. God wants to give us a heart without wounds and scars. Some of us have lived with those scars so long they are familiar and part of us. We have made them part of our identity. However, when we remain focused on our pain, we provide an opening for the enemy to come against us because we are dwelling on our hurt rather than trusting in His ability to heal us. Instead, by focusing on the truth of God's words and choosing to trust Him for our healing, we can close the door on the attacks of the enemy that wants to keep up oppressed and wounded.

> *I will give thanks and praise to You, for I am fearfully and wonderfully made;*
> *Wonderful are Your works, and my soul knows it very well. Psalm 139:14 AMP*

It has been said that hurting people hurt people. I imagine Father God is the first to cry when we are hurting, especially when we are hurt by people He created. One of our roles as representatives of Christ on earth is to be a witness of the love of our God. Through His healing our own hurt, we can offer a powerful testimony to the goodness of Jehovah Rophe. Then we share our victory with the hurting and the wounded that they might desire that same healing through Christ Jesus.

> *Praise be to the God and Father of our Lord Jesus Christ, the Father of compassion and the God of all comfort, who comforts us in all our troubles, so that we can comfort those in any trouble with the comfort we ourselves receive from God. 2 Corinthians 1:3-4 NIV*

> *He himself bore our sins in his body on the tree, that we might die to sin and live to righteousness. By his wounds you have been healed. 1 Peter 2:24 ESV*

Dr. Billy Graham said it this way:

When the Good Samaritan found a man robbed, beaten, and left for dead, he didn't continue on his trip and "report the accident." He didn't call 911 and leave the scene, nor pay someone else to go back and care for the man. The Samaritan himself got involved. He tenderly lifted the wounded body onto his own donkey and continued on the journey to Jericho. When he reached the city, he found a place to stay and probably cared for the patient. The next day, he made arrangements with the inn-keeper to pay all financial debts that the patient would incur. That is what bearing one another's burdens is all about. It's so easy to give to a charity or a ministry and feel good about it. It's not so easy to provide the personal charity. It's easier to give to someone overseas than it is to take a casserole next door. May God give us the sensitivity to recognize the needs of those around us and lend a helping hand.[10]

As victims, we often do not have full knowledge of God and His promises for us as His children. We battle fear, rejection, guilt, insecurity, and shame. As believers and survivors, one of our basic doctrines is the belief that the Bible is the written, inspired Word of God. It is God-breathed and living today.

For the word of God is alive and active. Sharper than any double-edged sword,
it penetrates even to dividing soul and spirit, joints and marrow;
it judges the thoughts and attitudes of the heart. Hebrews 4:12 NIV

All Scripture is given by inspiration of God, and is profitable for doctrine, for reproof,
for correction, for instruction in righteousness. 2 Timothy 3:16 KJV

Therefore, if the Bible is truth and what is written in the Bible is true, then what the Scriptures say about God and His promises are true. So, who is this God who wants to heal us?

WHO DOES GOD SAY HE IS?

Let's look at who God says He is using His own words.

1. Know therefore today, and take it to your heart, that the LORD, _____

_____

_____. Deuteronomy 4:39 NASB

2. _____

_____

_____. 1 Samuel 2:2 NASB

3. And he passed in front of Moses, proclaiming, _____

_____

_____

_____. Exodus 34:6 NIV

4. Bless the Lord, O my soul, and forget not all His benefits: _____

_____

_____

_____

_____. *Psalm 103:2-4 NKJV*

5. This is the message we have heard from him and declare to you: _____

_____

_____. *1 John 1:5 NIV*

6. Every good and perfect gift is from above, coming down from _____

_____

_____. *James 1:17 NIV*

7. Praise be to the Lord, to God _____

_____. *Psalm 68:19 NIV*

8. _____.

He is not a human, and _____

_____

_____. *Numbers 23:19 NCV*

9. For the LORD your God _____

_____

_____. *Deuteronomy 20:4 NIV*

10. Surely _____; *the Lord is* _____

_____. *Psalm 54:4 NIV*

11. _____

_____

_____.*1 Corinthians 1:9 NIV*

12. And so we know and rely on the love God has for us. _____

_____

_____. *1 John 4:16 NIV*

13. _____

_____

_____, *And He knows those who take refuge in Him. Nahum 1:7 NASB*

14. Behold, _____

_____

_____? Jeremiah 32:27 NKJV

15. _____

says the Lord God, _____

_____. Revelation 1:8 NASB

God wants us to reap the blessings that His names and attributes bring.

When we honor God's names, He will reveal His glory. God wants to be known. He longs for us to be in a relationship with Him. God wants us to reap the blessings that His names and attributes bring. His name is to be feared with the utmost reverence and loved with the greatest affection.[11]

GOD'S PROMISES

Now that we have a better understanding of who God is, what does He promise us as followers of Christ who have yielded our lives to Him? When we do our part, as noted in Scriptures, what is God faithful to do as His part?

1. _____

_____

_____. Psalm 50:15 NKJV

2. _____

_____. John 8:36 NKJV

3. _____

_____

_____

_____. Romans 8:1 NKJV

4. No temptation has overtaken you except such as is common to man; but _____

_____

_____

_____. 1 Corinthians 10:13 NKJV

5. _____

_____

_____. 2 Corinthians 5:17 NKJV

6. _____
_____
_____. *James 4:7 KJV*

7. _____
_____
_____
_____. *Isaiah 41:10 NKJV*

8. _____
_____. *Exodus 14:14 NLT*

9. _____
_____
_____. *Psalm 18:3 NKJV*

10. _____
_____
_____
_____
_____. *Isaiah 43:2 NKJV*

11. _____
_____
_____
_____. *John 14:27 NKJV*

12. _____
_____
_____. *Matthew 6:33 KJV*

13. _____
_____
_____. *Philippians 4:19 KJV*

14. _____
_____
_____. *Psalm 32:8 NIV*

15. _____
_____
_____. *Jeremiah 33:3 NKJV*

16. _____

_____

_____. *James 1:5 NIV*

17. _____

_____

_____

_____. *Isaiah 40:31 KJV*

18. _____

_____

_____. *This is the heritage of the servants*

of the Lord, and their righteousness is from Me, says the LORD. Isaiah 54:17 NKJV

19. *Being confident of this very thing, that* _____

_____

_____. *Philippians 1:6 KJV*

20. _____

_____. *Philippians 4:13 NKJV*

THE JOURNEY TO HEALING

Our journey to healing is progressive. It will take time, often years, and that's okay. Give yourself the same grace your Heavenly Father has extended to you. Some of us may still be on the road to complete healing even as we take our last breath on earth. I wish I could tell you it will be a quick work. The truth is that the damage caused by abuse is layers and layers deep, and each layer of hurt must be addressed. Until each hurt is addressed, you can never live the best life God has for you.

Our journey to healing is progressive.

So how do we begin our healing journey?

1. Start from a place of knowing God loves you, forgives you, accepts you, and wants to help you heal.

What then shall we say to these things? If God is for us,
who can be against us? Romans 8:31 NKJV

"For I know the plans I have for you," declares the Lord,
"plans to prosper you and not to harm you, plans to give
you hope and a future." Jeremiah 29:11 NIV

2. Ask the Holy Spirit to help you identify each area of your life that needs healing. Write them down as He reveals them to you.

He exposes even the darkest secrets. He sends light into
places that are as dark as death. Job 12:22 ERV

3. Speak the Word of God over each area He reveals.

The weapons we fight with are not the weapons of the world.
On the contrary, they have divine power to
demolish strongholds. 2 Corinthians 10:4 NIV

So will My word be which goes out of My mouth; it will not return to Me void [useless,
without result], without accomplishing what I desire, and without succeeding in the
matter for which I sent it. Isaiah 55:11 AMP

4. Release each broken area into the care of the great physician, Jesus, one at a time. When you can think about that person or that experience without feeling the hurt, move on to the next broken area. It's okay if you have to release the same person or experience more than once, even multiple times. Healing is a process.

Casting all your care upon Him, for He cares for you.
1 Peter 5:7 NKJV

5. Protect the broken areas (while you are waiting for the manifestation of your healing) from further harm by avoiding thoughts, people, and situations that may cause you additional harm.

The Lord is near to the brokenhearted and saves the
crushed in spirit. Psalm 34:18 ESV

6. Give thanks and rejoice as each broken area is healing.

Oh, give thanks to the Lord, for He is good! For His
mercy endures forever. 1 Chronicles 16:34 NKJV

7. Repeat the above steps as necessary.

For everything there is a season, and a time for
every matter under heaven. Ecclesiastes 3:1 ESV

Survivor: One Sunday at church, I found myself crying uncontrollably, and I didn't understand why. I had been out of my abusive relationship for quite a while. I had worked through so many hurts with the help of a support group, my friends, and much prayer. I had even forgiven him—several times! I thought I was pretty much past crying, yet here I was crying again. God told me I was grieving. "Grieving what?" I asked Him. "The loss of your dream." He showed me that I had never mourned the loss of the dream I had when we first married of living happily ever after. Although I had cried many angry and hurt tears when ending our marriage became necessary, I had never shed tears of sadness for the death of the future I thought our family would have. God, in His goodness, showed me I still needed healing, even when I didn't realize I did.

JOURNAL

Review the areas God showed you that need healing. Now write down Scriptures that you can speak over each one.

PRAYER

Heavenly Father, I come to You in the name of Jesus Christ, Your Son. You already know all about my wounded soul and spirit and my broken heart. Nothing that has happened to me has escaped Your attention. I choose now to release my hurts and wounds to You. I ask You to release me from each pain and heartache I have experienced at the hands of my abuser and others. I ask You to remove any desire in me to hold onto any of this pain. Help me rise up and know the joy and freedom of being made whole. I thank You that what the enemy meant for evil, You will turn to good. I choose now to accept my healing and wholeness. I thank You, Lord Jesus, that You hear and answer my cry. I give You all glory for You alone are worthy of all praise. In Your healing name, Jesus, I pray. Amen.

Lesson 8

HEALTHY RELATIONSHIPS

*And let us consider [thoughtfully] how we may encourage one another to love and
to do good deeds, not forsaking our meeting together [as believers for worship and
instruction], as is the habit of some, but encouraging one another; and all the more
[faithfully] as you see the day [of Christ's return] approaching.*
Hebrews 10:24-25 AMP

We all have relationships in our lives with family, friends, co-workers, acquaintances, neighbors, etc., but what constitutes a healthy relationship? We know abusive relationships are unhealthy, but many victims do not recognize that their marriage is abusive. They may acknowledge there is a problem but often cannot correctly identify the issues. It is not uncommon for victims to leave one abusive relationship and enter into another. By determining what constitutes a healthy relationship, we can make more informed choices before getting involved with someone. Recognizing "red flags" as indicators of unhealthy relationships can help us avoid abusive, controlling, or unequal relationships. God desires for us to have a healthy relationship with intimate partners, family, and friends.

*Finally, all of you be like-minded [united in spirit], sympathetic, brotherly,
kindhearted [courteous and compassionate toward each other as members
of one household], and humble in spirit. 1 Peter 3:8 AMP*

Survivor: Younger brother discussing me with his older brother: "The family has a few questions about your new girlfriend. She's pretty. She's smart. She's nice—so what's wrong with her?" What the younger brother didn't know was the years God had spent healing me from my abusive relationship. I didn't date; I worked on myself and my relationship with God. I had to find my identity as His child so that nothing any man ever did or said could affect me. I came to understand who He designed me to be so no man could alter me. I needed to be whole in Christ before I could enter another relationship. Before I could have a healthy relationship, I had to take the time to become healthy myself. It wasn't easy, but it was worth it.

CHARACTERISTICS OF A HEALTHY RELATIONSHIP

1. *Trust.* Partners are able to place trust in each other and give each other the benefit of the doubt. Partners are comfortable with the other participating in activities separate from them.

2. *Safety.* Physical, emotional, and financial safety are musts in every healthy relationship.

3. *Mutual respect.* Partners genuinely value who the other is. Opinions and feelings are listened to, and boundaries are honored.

4. *Honesty.* Fully sharing truthful information builds trust and strengthens the relationship.

5. *Compromise.* In any relationship, each partner does not always get his or her way. Each acknowledges different points of view and is willing to give and take as long as the compromise does not result in unhealthy or dangerous actions.

6. *Individuality.* Partners do not have to compromise who God created them to be. Their identities should not be based on their partner's identity. Both should continue seeing their friends and doing the things they love. Both should be supportive of their partner wanting to pursue new interests or make new friends.

7. *Good communication.* Each partner speaks honestly and openly to avoid miscommunication. Each partner should respect the other's wishes to sort out feelings and wait a reasonable time before continuing the conversation.

Before we can have a healthy relationship, we have to take the time to become healthy ourselves.

8. *Anger control.* Anger is to be handled in healthy ways. We all get angry, but how we express our anger can affect our relationships with others.

9. *Fighting fair.* Everyone argues at some point. To promote the likelihood of coming up with a possible solution, stick to the subject, avoid insults, and refrain from blaming. Partners agree to take a short break away from each other if the discussion gets too heated.

10. *Problem solving.* Partners can learn to solve problems and identify new solutions by breaking a problem into small parts or by talking through the situation. Admitting wrongs and accepting responsibility for one's actions is important.

11. *Understanding.* Each partner should take time to understand what the other might be thinking and feeling.

12. *Self-confidence.* When partners have true confidence in themselves, it can help their relationships with others. It shows that they are calm and comfortable enough to allow others to express their opinions without forcing their own opinions on them.

13. *Being a role model.* By embodying what respect means, partners can inspire each other, friends, and family to behave considerately. Showing respect is an important way to promote healthy relationships in future generations.

14. *Healthy sexual relationship.* Partners engage in a sexual relationship that both are comfortable with, and neither partner feels pressured or forced to engage in sexual activity outside his or her comfort zone.[12]

15. *Growth.* Healthy relationships are nurtured rather than left stagnant from neglect. Partners accept that change is a natural part of every healthy relationship.

16. *Commitment.* Partners work together to ensure the relationship is healthy and satisfying for both of them.

HEALTHY RELATIONSHIPS

Rank the importance of each healthy relationship trait from 1 to 16 on the puzzle pieces. Number 1 will be your highest priority. Below, list your top 5 traits.

1._____

2._____

3._____

4._____

5._____

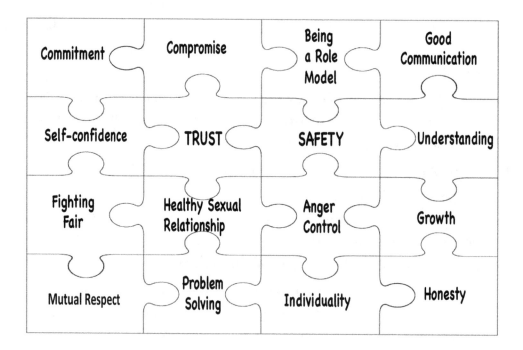

Why do you think TRUST and SAFETY are capitalized in the puzzle? _____

_____

Survivor: The thought of being in a newrelationship elevated my anxiety. I remember having a conversation with God about my future. I told God I was fine with it just being Him and me. But if that was not His plan for me, He would have to bring the person to me because I wasn't going out looking. Then I proceeded to write down exactly what I wanted in a partner. I mean, I wrote down two pages of things! I wrote down everything important to me in a relationship, from honesty and integrity to love of family and valuing me, from being a man after God's own heart and a worshiper to his physical characteristics and need to have handyman abilities. I wrote it all down. I realized until I knew what I was looking for in a mate, I wouldn't recognize it when he came my way—and he did. God really does give us the desires of our heart. (Psalm 37:4)

RELATIONSHIP RIGHTS

Both parties share the same rights. Individual rights do not threaten healthy relationships.

1. I have the right to stay true to who God created me to be.

2. I have the right to continue to grow and change as a Christian and as a person.

3. I have the right to seek help, if needed, without being criticized for it.

4. I have the right to live free from all types of coercion, intimidation, violence, and abuse.

5. I have a right to healthy love and to be loved in a healthy manner.

6. I have a right to enjoy all the fruits of the spirit: love, joy, peace, patience, kindness, goodness, faithfulness, gentleness, and self-control. (Galatians 5: 22-23)

7. I have a right to be valued and respected.

8. I have a right to live without shame, blame, or guilt.

9. I have a right to feel and express my emotions.

10. I have a right to maintain [nonsexual] relationships apart from my partner.

11. I have the right to expect honesty and trust.

12. I have the right to express my opinions and have my opinions respected, even those that may differ from my partner's.

13. I have the right to pursue activities without my partner or to refuse to participate in activities I don't enjoy.

14. I have the right to have my decisions respected, even if I change my mind.

15. I have the right to set and enforce boundaries and to privacy.

16. I have the right to be imperfect.

17. I have the right to change my feelings toward someone.

18. I have the right to separate from unhealthy relationships.

QUESTIONS:

Write the numbers of the statements that answer each question.

1. Which rights do you struggle to believe are yours? _____

_____

2. Which rights are difficult to expect from your family? _____

_____

3. Which rights are difficult to expect from your friends? _____

_____

4. Which rights do you struggle to honor with your family? _____

_____

5. Which rights do you struggle to honor with your friends? _____

_____

6. What additional rights do you think should be added to the list? _____

_____

_____

_____

_____

_____

_____

RELATIONSHIP RED FLAGS

Red flags are the warning signs that the person you are in a relationship with, or are contemplating a relationship with, may be potentially abusive. A few signs can show there is potential for abuse. The more signs a person possesses, the more likely the person is abusive.

1. Is overly involved in partner's daily life

2. Desires to "fast track" the relationship

3. Presents as rescuer/protector

4. Expresses strong opinions/beliefs

5. Violates individual rights and boundaries

6. Makes all decisions

7. Monitors partner's whereabouts, activities, spending

8. Displays extreme jealousy/possessiveness

9. Makes unfounded accusations

10. Has bitterness/unresolved past relationship issues

11. Has history of stalking

12. Has history of trouble with law enforcement/fighting

13. Exhibits explosive temper

14. Makes threats of violence

15. Displays hypersensitivity/overreactions

16. Minimizes/disregards partner's feelings/opinions

17. Dismisses partner's problems/concerns/needs as irritational/unimportant

18. Has poor family/friend relationships

19. Isolates partner from others

20. Is self-centered

21. Exhibits immaturity/emotional insecurity/dependency

22. Displays most emotions as anger; difficulty conveying other emotions

23. Has false sense of superiority masking low self-esteem

24. Feels entitled to treat others as inferior

25. Becomes angry if wishes are not anticipated and fulfilled

26. Makes constant putdowns/belittling comments

27. Has frequent anger/hostility toward someone/something

28. Has extreme personality changes (Jekyll/Hyde)

29. Behaves very differently around others than when alone with partner

30. Is unable to communicate in a healthy way

31. Is closed to criticism or suggestions

32. Uses force during arguments

33. Expects advice/orders to be followed

34. Has unspoken/ever-changing rules

35. Expects unwavering loyalty

36. Makes promises with no follow-through

37. Exhibits double standard of behavior/male supremacy

38. Fails to be truthful/honest

39. Is unable to trust or be trusted

40. Makes cruel/derogatory comments passed off as "teasing"

41. Displays cruelty to children/animals

42. Has current or past abusive/violent behavior

43. Had aggressive/delinquent behavior as a youth

44. Witnessed IPV as a child

45. Was physically/psychologically abused as a child

46. Minimizes abusive behavior and its effects on others

47. Has a pattern of instability/conflict in relationships

48. Plays the victim/seeks sympathy

49. Family/friends have concerns

50. Uses "playful" force during sex

51. Coerces sex, alcohol/drug use

52. Treats others disrespectfully

53. Displays anger about someone/something often

54. Blames others for his problems/feelings

55. Is unpredictable

56. Has unrealistic expectations

57. Exhibits controlling/manipulative behavior

58. Excuses/rationalizes/justifies behavior

59. Displays antisocial or borderline/narcissistic personality traits

60. Believes he is blameless

61. Believes rules/consequences don't apply to him

62. Takes financial advantage of partner

63. Has history of unemployment/getting fired

64. Seeks financial control over partner

65. Exhibits heavy drug/alcohol use

66. Is unwilling to make/keep commitments

67. Is frequently unfaithful

68. Displays attitudes accepting/justifying abuse

69. Exhibits cultural acceptance of violence

70. Displays hostility toward women

71. Has ongoing depression

72. Makes threats of suicide

73. Is secretive about past alluding to addictions/illegal behavior

74. Desires power and control in relationships

75. Gets what he wants one way or another

Read the following passage and see how many possible relationship red flags you can find.

I met my abuser through my family's business. He was tall, dark, and handsome with loads of charisma. He was the type of man that women turned to admire as he walked confidently across the room. He was often the center of attention, telling stories that kept his audience entertained for hours.

My family told me he was a womanizer. I declined going out with him for months because he had a longtime girlfriend, even though he asked persistently. He finally told me he had broken up with her because she was unstable and on drugs. He called her a real "B word" often. I found out too late that he had beaten her and put her in the hospital. Her family intervened.

I still kept declining to go out because I knew he drank a lot. When he accepted a job requiring him to move out of state, I finally agreed to have dinner with him because he "really just needed someone to talk to" and knew I helped others. There was the hook: he wanted me to help him. I was duly flattered. He shared an awful family secret and told me I was the only one who was on his side, the only one who understood.

What began as a goodbye talk turned into spending all our free time together before he left. He knew my family already but introduced me to his and even came to church with me. Looking back, I can pinpoint the first time he crossed a boundary I had set. He became aggravated because I wouldn't change my mind, and he threatened to leave. I panicked, thinking he was going to leave, and changed my mind and agreed with him. I was already becoming a "pleaser" rather than risk conflict or lose him.

How many red flags did you find?_____

QUESTIONS:

1. Which of any red flag behaviors do or did you recognize in your abuser? _____

_____

_____

_____

_____

2. Which of any red flag behaviors do or did you recognize in previous or current relationships? _____

_____

_____

_____

_____

3. How can you address red flags in your relationships? _____

_____

_____

_____

_____

Do not be yoked together with unbelievers. For what do righteousness and
wickedness have in common? Or what fellowship can light have with darkness?
2 Corinthians 6:14 NIV

KINDS OF RELATIONSHIP LOVE

Not all love is the healthy kind. It is important to recognize when we are currently involved in or are heading for the unhealthy kind of love.

During the romantic love phase, everything seems perfect. Both partners put their best foot forward. They may spend a lot of time together. Unattractive traits may be ignored or redefined: he is determined, not stubborn; devoted, not possessive. Eventually, both partners see the faults of the other. At that point, the relationship can grow into a healthy, nurturing relationship or an unhealthy, addictive one.

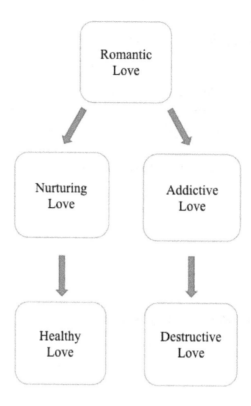

Nurturing love evolves from romantic love that matures into a deeper, more complex relationship. Both partners grow as individuals with the encouragement of their partners. Both accept each other's limitations. They encourage close friendships and relationships with others. They encourage each other's satisfaction with independent activities. Should the relationship end, sadness and grief are expected reactions. Neither party will be devastated to the point of self-destruction or being unable to function.

Addictive love occurs when romantic love turns into an extreme need for one partner, usually the potential victim, to be constantly available. Increasingly, less of the couple's time together is satisfying, joyful, or interesting. Increasingly, more of the couple's time together is spent arguing, making promises, apologizing, expressing anger, feeling guilty, and being afraid of upsetting the other person. As a result, self-worth and self-control diminish. The woman narrows her focus to concentrate on pleasing her partner. She develops an inflated idea of her partner's importance to her and her importance to him. The relationship becomes exclusive, focusing only on each other. Individual growth and maturity are stunted. As the woman acts more emotionally needy, the man increases his efforts to control her. The woman relinquishes her power to make healthy choices.

QUESTIONS:

1. Define romantic love. _____
_____

2. Define nurturing love. _____
_____
_____

3. Define addictive love. _____
_____
_____
_____

HOW HEALTHY IS YOUR RELATIONSHIP?

As you read through the following statements, mark the ones that are generally present in your relationships.

1. We place God at the head of our relationship.

2. We trust each other.

3. We treat each other with respect.

4. We treat each other's opinions with respect.

5. We encourage each other in our respective endeavors.

6. We honor our commitments to each other.

7. We both have some decision-making power about what we do in the relationship.

8. We both have some say in financial matters.

9. We both accept responsibility for our actions.

10. We resolve conflicts without cursing, yelling, or insults.

11. We both apologize when we are wrong.

12. We both have some privacy with electronic devices and technology.

13. We allow each other time alone.

14. We enjoy spending time together, with our own friends, and with each other's friends.

15. We have close friends and family who are happy about our relationship.

16. We always feel safe with each other.

17. We accept changes in the relationship.

18. We never feel pressured for sex.

QUESTIONS:

Write the numbers of the statements that answer each question.

1. Which statements are most prevalent in your current relationship with your partner?

_____

_____

2. Which statements are most prevalent in relationships with your family and friends?

_____

_____

3. What areas are or may have been problems in your relationships? _____

_____

_____

STARTING NEW RELATIONSHIPS

The recommended time for healing from any relationship is a minimum of six months for every year of the relationship. Once time has passed and you are ready to take a step in starting a new dating relationship, here is a list of suggestions.

1. Do feel confident in who you are.

2. Do meet in public places for the first several dates.

3. Do start with non-threatening activities.

4. Do share honestly about who you are and what you want in a relationship.

5. Do notice common interests.

6. Do ask about likes and dislikes.

7. Do ask about family, friends, and past relationships.

8. Do ask about values and beliefs.

9. Do ask about goals and dreams.

10. Do use caution when meeting people on the internet.

11. Do trust your instincts about being safe.

12. Do bring your own money and be prepared to pay.

13. Do take time to get to know each other well.

14. Do watch and listen for red flags.

15. Do use caution when introducing your new partner to your children.

16. Do ask trusted family and friends for their opinion of your new partner.

17. Do tell someone who you'll be with and where you're going.

18. Do keep your boundaries in place.

Survivor: I finally started dating again after years, I wouldn't even tell the man I was seeing from months where I lived. It was easier to avoid the problem than to see if I was really able to set boundaries. It would have been a red flag had he pressured me to tell him where I lived before I was ready, but he didn't. I also let him know I was running his name through a criminal database. When we talked on the phone, I asked him questions I got from Christian websites about healthy relationships and compatibility, over 250 of them! It's a wonder he stuck around.

19. Don't play games; tell him if you are interested or not.

20. Don't get drunk or high to "loosen up" or feel confident on a date.

21. Don't get into a car alone or become isolated with people you don't know.

22. Don't go alone to other people's homes or invite people you just met to your home.

23. Don't introduce your new dating partner to your children too soon.

24. Don't leave your children alone with your new dating partner.

25. Don't monopolize the conversation talking about your ex.

26. Don't send mixed messages, especially about sex.

27. Don't do anything you don't want to do, including anything sexual.

28. Don't pretend to be someone you are not so he will like you.

29. Don't judge him based on your past relationships.

30. Don't share too much too fast.

JOURNAL

Write down what a healthy relationship would look like for you. What steps can you begin taking now to have healthier relationships?

PRAYER

Father God, how grateful I am that I don't have to be vigilant in looking for red flags in my relationship with You. Your relationship with me is a model of how healthy relationships should be. As I move forward adding new people to my life, I ask that You increase my discernment. Show me the hidden things that I need to know about new people. If those people are not healthy for me, please get my attention and let me know. I commit to keeping You at the center of all my relationships. In the amazing name of Jesus I pray, Amen.

Lesson 9

BOUNDARIES

So then each of us will give an account of himself to God. Romans 14:12 ESV

One of the common difficulties women who have been abused face is the inability to set and enforce boundaries with the people in their lives, especially with their partners, children, family, and friends. Boundaries are simply the rules or expectations for a relationship or situation that help restore your personal power. Your physical boundaries are violated when someone stands too close or takes food from your plate. Your emotional boundaries are violated when someone presumes to know how you feel, what you should do, or how you should think.

For women who are abused, setting boundaries can be a matter of safety. By setting boundaries, we help ourselves and help others understand what is acceptable and safe and what is not, what is our responsibility and what is not. Setting and enforcing personal boundaries shows you have enough respect for yourself and others to discourage inappropriate and harmful behavior.

How do you know your boundaries are being violated? Check your body. Your body will signal you that your power is being stripped. Your internal warning system will activate. Unhealthy boundaries can result in feeling pressured, stressed, anxious, fearful, manipulated, bullied, exploited, controlled, angry, overwhelmed, weak, helpless, desperate, guilty, shamed, and tired.

Survivor: I didn't realize I had a problem setting boundaries until we talked about it in group one night. It really hit me that I wanted to please people so much I allowed them to ignore my feelings and opinions, my wants and needs. It wasn't just with my ex I had problems—it was with coworkers, supervisors, family, and friends. I didn't want to create a fuss in the family by disagreeing. I didn't want people not to like me. I didn't want to be seen as a b-word at work or as uncooperative. It was terrifying for me to have a confrontation. My heart would race, my face would drain of color, and I would get physically ill. I usually cried afterward. How did I get like that?

GOD MODELED BOUNDARIES

1. God established boundaries in the Garden of Eden with Adam and Eve.

And the LORD God commanded the man, saying, "Of every tree of the garden you may freely eat; but of the tree of the knowledge of good and evil you shall not eat, for in the day that you eat of it you shall surely die." Genesis 2:16-17 NKJV

When Adam and Eve respected God's boundaries and avoided eating from the tree of the knowledge of good and evil, they were able to enjoy fullness of life with God. When they violated God's boundaries, their relationship with God changed, and they would return to dust in death. (Genesis 3:19)

2. God established boundaries with the Ten Commandments in the book of Exodus.

¹ And God spoke all these words: ² "I am the Lord your God, who brought you out of Egypt, out of the land of slavery. ³ You shall have no other gods before me. ⁴ You shall not make for yourself an image in the form of anything in heaven above or on the earth beneath or in the waters below. ⁵ You shall not bow down to them or worship them; for I, the Lord your God, am a jealous God, punishing the children for the sin of the parents to the third and fourth generation of those who hate me, ⁶ but showing love to a thousand generations of those who love me and keep my commandments. ⁷ You shall not misùse the name of the Lord your God, for the Lord will not hold anyone guiltless who misuses his name. ⁸ Remember the Sabbath day by keeping it holy. ⁹ Six days you shall labor and do all your work, ¹⁰ but the seventh day is a sabbath to the Lord your God. On it you shall not do any work, neither you, nor your son or daughter, nor your male or female servant, nor your animals, nor any foreigner residing in your towns. ¹¹ For in six days the Lord made the heavens and the earth, the sea, and all that is in them, but he rested on

the seventh day. Therefore the Lord blessed the Sabbath day and made it holy. [12] Honor your father and your mother, so that you may live long in the land the Lord your God is giving you. [13] You shall not murder. [14] You shall not commit adultery. [15] You shall not steal. [16] You shall not give false testimony against your neighbor. [17] You shall not covet your neighbor's house. You shall not covet your neighbor's wife, or his male or female servant, his ox or donkey, or anything that belongs to your neighbor."
Exodus 20:1-17 NIV

In verses 3-11, God sets the boundaries on how He expects to be treated. In verse 12, He sets the boundary for how parents are to be treated. In verses 13-17, He sets the boundaries for how others are to be treated, especially neighbors.

3. Jesus set boundaries when the crowds pressed in as His fame for healing spread. He stayed focused on what God had called Him to do, not what others expected Him to do.

Yet the news about him spread all the more, so that crowds of people came to hear him and to be healed of their sicknesses. But Jesus often withdrew to lonely places and prayed.
Luke 5:15-16 NIV

4. Jesus set and enforced the boundary for how to treat God's house respectfully when the money changers were disrespecting it.

The Passover of the Jews was at hand, and Jesus went up to Jerusalem. In the temple he found those who were selling oxen and sheep and pigeons, and the money-changers sitting there. And making a whip of cords, he drove them all out of the temple, with the sheep and oxen. And he poured out the coins of the money-changers and overturned their tables. And he told those who sold the pigeons, "Take these things away; do not make my Father's house a house of trade." John 2:13-16 ESV

5. Jesus set boundaries with His disciples regarding the treatment of children.

Then children were brought to him that he might lay his hands on them and pray. The disciples rebuked the people, but Jesus said, "Let the little children come to me and do not hinder them, for to such belongs the kingdom of heaven." And he laid his hands on them and went away. Matthew 19:13-15 ESV

6. Jesus quickly addressed a situation by letting Peter know he had crossed a boundary.

And he began to teach them that the Son of Man must suffer many things and be rejected by the elders and the chief priests and the scribes and be killed, and after three days rise again. And he said this plainly. And Peter took him aside and began to rebuke him. But turning and seeing his disciples, he rebuked Peter and said, "Get behind me, Satan! For you are not setting your mind on the things of God, but on the things of man."
Mark 8:31-33 ESV

ADVANTAGES OF SETTING BOUNDARIES

Taking responsibility for our own lives is freeing. We can focus on what is important to us instead of what others want to be important to us. We are free to follow the leading of the Holy Spirit and not the demands of man.

Teach me to do your will, for you are my God! Let your good
Spirit lead me on level ground! Psalm 143:10 ESV

If we are doing for others out of love, we should have joy. If we are doing for others out of fear, there will be no joy. It is our job to guard our hearts. It takes wisdom and discernment to know what things we should be doing and what things we shouldn't. We must create and maintain invisible hedges around our physical and spiritual lives and our mental and emotional lives.

Guard your heart above all else, for it determines the course of your life.
Proverbs 4:23 NLT

Setting boundaries is helpful for healthy relationships. Lack of boundaries or unhealthy boundaries can attract those who will take advantage of you.

1. Setting boundaries define what is our responsibility and what is the responsibility of others. We are on a path designed by God. Our very steps are ordered by Him. Without boundaries, we get sidetracked off that ordained path.

The steps of a good man are ordered by the Lord,
and He delights in his way. Psalm 37:23 NKJV

Trust in the Lord with all your heart, and do not lean
on your own understanding. In all your ways acknowledge him,
and he will make straight your paths. Proverbs 3:5-6 ESV

2. Setting boundaries helps us keep our priorities straight. We cannot please both God and man. Our desire should be to complete the work God set before us and not be detoured by man's work.

> *No servant can serve two masters. Either he will hate*
> *the one and love the other, or he will be devoted to*
> *the one and despise the other. Luke 16:13 ESV*

> *But more than anything else, put God's work first*
> *and do what he wants. Then the other things*
> *will be yours as well. Matthew 6:33 CEV*

3. Setting boundaries helps model healthy relationships for our children. Poor boundaries affect our relationships inside and outside our families. We teach our children to expect things right now. They witness others expecting us to drop everything and help them with their problems or crisis of their own making with little respect for our time and energy. Naturally, our children want us to do the same for them. We get to be known as the "go-to" person if anyone has a need, which may sound great, but in the long run, is not. Our stress from the negative emotions of resentment, anger, and frustration causes the release of toxins in our bodies. This same pattern of behavior may be present in our children if we don't make a change.

Setting boundaries is helpful for healthy relationships.

> *I have taught you in the way of wisdom; I have led*
> *you in right paths. Proverbs 4:11 NKJV*

4. Setting boundaries helps those around us to experience the natural consequences of their poor choices, hopefully creating a desire to change. With poor boundaries, we often spare others difficulty and fail to allow them to reap the ramifications of their actions. We do not allow others to develop the skills they need to solve their own problems because we rescue them.

> *One with great rage will pay a penalty. For if you rescue him,*
> *you will have to do it again. Proverbs 19:19 TLV*

> **Survivor**: I had an opportunity to speak to a group of men in a batterers program. After sharing pieces of my story, we had a time of questions and answers. One man asked me, "You said he did all that? What did you do?" At first, I thought he was blaming me. Then he clarified he was asking about my response to the abuse. I answered, "I didn't do anything. I was too scared! He was bigger than me and stronger than me. If I couldn't escape, I just tried to be invisible and hope he wouldn't notice me. I had a child to protect." The man leaned back in his chair and crossed his arms before responding. "You didn't do anything? Well, that's the problem. That man didn't have any consequences. He's not going to stop. Why should he? Nothing happens to him when he does that." His answer was like a punch in the stomach, taking my breath. After a moment of silence, I had to ask, "What should I have done?" He leaned forward, "Leave. You should have left. You don't need to put up with that sh*t." Other men in the group nodded in agreement. This advice is from the very men who are abusers.

If repercussions are not experienced when boundaries and consequences are clearly understood, the people violating the boundary have no need to change their behavior. God demonstrates this kind of consequence with Israel.

> *I will return again to My place till they acknowledge their offense. Then they will seek My face; in their affliction they will earnestly seek Me. Hosea 5:15 NKJV*

A common frustration heard from victims of abuse is the ability of their abusers to talk themselves out of any penalties for their abusive behavior. Most abusers are experts at manipulating others. If the court chooses to dismiss charges or give him another chance, he has escaped the consequences of breaking boundaries that were set by legal statutes. He feels above the law. He has no need to change because there are no consequences for his actions.

Setting boundaries helps us avoid unhealthy relationships.

> *Do not be deceived: God cannot be mocked. A man reaps what he sows. Whoever sows to please their flesh, from the flesh will reap destruction; whoever sows to please the Spirit, from the Spirit will reap eternal life. Galatians 6:7-8 NIV*

5. Setting boundaries helps us avoid unhealthy relationships. While we can't change someone else's poor behavior, we can limit our exposure to it.

Whoever walks with the wise becomes wise, but the companion of fools will suffer harm.
Proverbs 13:20 ESV

6. Setting boundaries helps us keep our peace. Sometimes we have to keep our peace from waaaaaay far away.

If possible, as far as it depends on you, live at peace with everyone. Romans 12:18 AMP

SOME REASONS WE DON'T SET BOUNDARIES

There may be many reasons for failing to set boundaries.[13]

1. We may fear others will see us as self-centered or selfish and feel guilty about saying no. As stewards of the life God gifted us, we want to be protective of that life and the time God has given us.

The Spirit of God has made me, and the breath of the
Almighty gives me life. Job 33:4 ESV

2. We may fear others will see us as rude or as hurting someone's feelings.

Casting all your cares [all your anxieties, all your worries, and all your concerns, once
and for all] on Him, for He cares about you [with deepest affection,
and watches over you very carefully]. 1 Peter 5:7 AMP

3. We may fear rejection and being alone if we don't please people.

I will make My dwelling among you, and My soul will not reject
nor separate itself from you. Leviticus 26:11 AMP

4. We may fear conflict and want to keep the peace.

And the peace of God [that peace which reassures the heart, that peace] which
transcends all understanding, [that peace which] stands guard over your hearts and
your minds in Christ Jesus [is yours]. Philippians 4:7 AMP

5. We may fear we are not doing the "right" or "Christian" thing.

There is no fear in love, but perfect love casts out fear.
For fear has to do with punishment, and whoever fears
has not been perfected in love. 1 John 4:18 ESV

6. We may feel disloyal or unloving to our abusive husbands.

> *It [love] does not rejoice at wrongdoing,*
> *but rejoices with the truth. 1 Corinthians 13:6 ESV*

7. We may enjoy the praise we get for being "superwoman."

> *For they loved the praise of men more than the praise of God. John 12:43 KJV*

By failing to set boundaries, we remain at the beck and call of others. By failing to set boundaries, we may appear generous, unselfish, polite, helpful, easy-going, dependable, and capable. However, unhealthy boundaries often lead to our own secret resentment, stress, and exhaustion.

Sometimes the pressure to give in comes from others and what they want us to do: he *made* me. Sometimes the pressure comes from inside us and what we think we should do: I *had* to. Making decisions based on the praise or rejection of man is responding in the flesh. Making decisions based on guilt is also responding to the flesh. God instructs us to pay attention to our Spirit, not our flesh.

> *God instructs us to pay attention to our Spirit, not our flesh.*

> *For if you live according to the flesh you will die, but if by the Spirit you*
> *put to death the deeds of the body, you will live. Romans 8:13 ESV*

It is true the Bible in Galatians talks about helping others with their burdens.

> *¹Brothers, if anyone is caught in any sin, you who are spiritual [that is, you who are responsive to the guidance of the Spirit] are to restore such a person in a spirit of gentleness [not with a sense of superiority or self-righteousness], keeping a watchful eye on yourself, so that you are not tempted as well. ² Carry one another's burdens and in this way you will fulfill the requirements of the law of Christ [that is, the law of Christian love]. ³ For if anyone thinks he is something [special] when [in fact] he is nothing [special except in his own eyes], he deceives himself. ⁴ But each one must carefully scrutinize his own work [examining his actions, attitudes, and behavior], and then he can have the personal satisfaction and inner joy of doing something commendable without comparing himself to another. ⁵ For every person will have to bear [with patience] his own burden*

[of faults and shortcomings for which he alone is responsible].
Galatians 6:1-5 AMP

In verse 1, the Apostle Paul is speaking in the context of bearing the burdens of Believers who need to be restored from mistakes, not of the deliberate, hardened sinner who has no desire to change. The sin is acknowledged, not ignored or excused. In verse 2, he references helping those who have fallen into sin get back on track without adding to their heaviness with condemnation and judgment. He is clear that we are not to stay in the place of continually being overtaken by the same sin. When Paul speaks of bearing our own load in verse 5, he refers to each of us as Christians being answerable to God for our own personal decisions. No one can carry the load of our Christian walk but us.

Also, the word *load* has different meanings in each verse. In verse 2, load means "heavy burdens" as those too heavy to carry alone. In verse 5, *load* was a common term for a soldier's backpack, implying things the bearer can carry. We are not expected to carry the burdens of others that they can carry themselves. It may be that the person who reminds you that we are to help carry each other's burdens is trying to manipulate you into helping. Use your discernment, as you are never meant to be manipulated by God's Word. Burdens that create a crisis because others didn't do what they were supposed to do or made no effort to plan ahead are not your responsibility. We're talking about a pattern of behavior where the other person feels entitled to have their needs met at the expense of your time, energy, and resources.

PRACTICING BOUNDARIES

Setting boundaries that make your position clear can be easier if you prepare "go-to" statements when confronted with a situation that makes you uncomfortable. Essentially, state your rehearsed "go-to" words to whatever the other person says without ever changing the phrasing. You might have seen this practice demonstrated on courtroom drama shows where the witness repeatedly states, "On the advice of counsel, I exercise my fifth amendment rights," or "I don't recall that event."

The words may not always fit what the other person is saying, but say them anyway. Speak calmly and firmly with little emotion. The point is to send the message that you will not be changing your mind. When some people perceive a weakening of your resolve, it becomes easier for them to override your objections and violate your boundary, so stick to your prepared script.

Examples:

1. I won't be participating/helping.

"Our women's club needs a couple more members."

"I won't be participating."

"It'll be lots of fun. You know almost everybody there."

"I won't be participating."

"I'm in charge of getting new members, and I really need you to come."

"I won't be participating."

"I thought we were friends."

"I won't be participating."

2. I'm not available/My time is already committed.

"I know you said you were busy, but I have to be out of my apartment today."

"I'm not available."

"But I have a lot of stuff to move!"

"I'm not available."

"You seriously are not going to help me?"

"I'm not available."

"I thought I could count on my sister."

"I'm not available."

3. It sounds as if you have a problem.

"Mom, I need supplies for my project that's due tomorrow."

"It sounds as if you have a problem."

"I need you to get these supplies tonight."

"It sounds as if you have a problem."

"Mom! I have to have these supplies!"

"It sounds as if you have a problem."

"Mom, I'll get an F if I don't turn it in!"

"It sounds as if you have a problem."

4. I'm not comfortable with that.

"I need to come get my tools."

"I'm not comfortable with that."

"They're my f***ing tools!"

"I'm not comfortable with that."

"I'm coming over!"

"I'm not comfortable with that."
"You can't keep my tools!"
"I'm not comfortable with that."

5. The courts will decide.

"You're not getting the house!"
"The courts will decide."
"There's no way I'm paying that much child support!"
"The courts will decide."
"And you're not getting the truck."
"The courts will decide."
"I'm getting custody of the kids!"
"The courts will decide."

6. I respect your right to feel that way.

"No piece of paper is going to keep me from my kids!"
"I respect your right to feel that way."
"You're going to be sorry!"
"I respect your right to feel that way."
"You are such a f***ing b*tch!"
"I respect your right to feel that way."
"You better let me see my kids!"
"I respect your right to feel that way."

7. If that's what you feel you need to do.

"I'm going to tell everybody what you've done!"
"If that's what you feel you need to do."
"Everybody in your precious church is going to know what a hypocrite you are."
"If that's what you feel you need to do."
"They won't let you in the doors when I'm through."
"If that's what you feel you need to do."

8. I've already answered that question.

"Can I pretty please stay out an hour past curfew?"
"I've already answered that question."
"Why not? You know he's a safe driver."
"I've already answered that question."

"But, Mom, I told him I could go, and he wants to stay out later."

"I've already answered that question."

"You're so mean!"

"I've already answered that question."

9. I'm not going to discuss this.

"Why is he saying you cheated on him?"

"I'm not going to discuss this."

"He says you are the one who moved out."

"I'm not going to discuss this."

"Why don't you go to counseling and work out your problems."

"I'm not going to discuss this."

"How can you just throw it all away?"

"I'm not going to discuss this."

"What about your kids?"

"I'm not going to discuss this."

10. I won't change my mind/I'm not changing my mind.

"Why do you have to go back to college now?"

"I'm not changing my mind."

"You can always go next semester."

"I'm not changing my mind."

"But what about your job?"

"I'm not changing my mind."

"You're wasting your time and money."

"I'm not changing my mind."

11. My answer is no.

"You need to drop that restraining order."

"My answer is no."

"I said I was sorry."

"My answer is no."

"Just let me come back home and everything will be fine."

"My answer is no."

"The kids need their daddy."

"My answer is no."

12. I will follow the court order as it is written.

"I know it's your weekend, but I need to switch again."

"I will follow the court order as it is written."

"Why do you have to be such a selfish b*tch?"

"I will follow the court order as it is written."

"Why can't you cut me some f***king slack so I can go fishing with the guys?"

"I will follow the court order as it is written."

13. I'm sticking to my decision.

"I know you are dieting, but this chocolate cake was on sale."

"I'm sticking to my decision."

"You can just have a little piece."

"I'm sticking to my decision."

"I already bought it, so you have to eat it."

"I'm sticking to my decision."

14. I have to get going/I have to get this done/Now is not a good time.

"Have you seen that new movie?"

"I have to get this done."

"It's the one with that actor you really like."

"I have to get this done."

"I just thought you'd like it."

"I have to get this done."

"We'll only be gone a few hours."

"I have to get this done."

15. That's not your decision to make.

"You need to take him back."

"That's not your decision to make."

"Kids need their father."

"That's not your decision to make."

"He's not drinking anymore."

"That's not your decision to make."

"You're being too hard on him."

"That's not your decision to make."

Here is a list of "go-to" statements you can use.

1. I'm sorry you feel that way.

2. I'm not comfortable/okay with that.

3. That doesn't work for me.

4. I need you to respect my boundaries.

5. I won't be doing that.

6. I don't agree.

7. I don't feel comfortable doing that.

8. It sounds as if you have a problem.

9. I won't be solving your problem.

10. I already have plans.

11. I'm not available.

12. I won't be participating/helping.

13. I need to think about what I want to do.

14. I won't give you an answer now.

15. I have to get this done.

16. Now is not a good time.

17. I'm not able to take that on right now.

18. My time is already committed.

19. I am unable to help at this time.

20. I'm unable to make that big of a commitment right now.

21. I don't feel comfortable discussing this.

22. I'm not going to discuss this with you.

23. I won't change my mind.

24. I need to honor my commitments to my family.

25. I've already answered that question.

26. I said, "No."

27. Please stop.

28. I have made my decision.

29. I respect your right to feel that way.

30. If that's what you feel you need to do.

31. I'm sticking to what I said.

32. Please say that in a different way.

33. You are violating my boundary.

34. Please stop disrespecting my wishes/decisions.

35. Talk to my attorney/the court.

36. I will follow the court order as it is written.

37. I won't be responding to your calls/texts/messages/emails.

38. That's not your decision to make.

39. I will make that decision.

40. I will ask for your help when I need it.

ROLE-PLAY 1

Now go back and role-play a few of the previous 1-15 scenarios with a partner using different "go-to" statements. Take turns being the person saying the "go-to" statements. You may want to prepare by standing tall and appearing confident (Superman pose) before speaking your "go-to" statements. It really can help. Discuss the activity afterward.

After your boundaries are well established, you may want to soften or willingly choose to expand your response a bit for those people with whom you would like to continue having a positive, healthy relationship.

1. Instead of just saying, "I'm not comfortable with that," you might add, "but I am comfortable with this."

2. Instead of just saying, "I won't be helping," you might add, "but I could help next month."

3. Instead of just saying, "I won't be solving your problem," you might add, "but I'm willing to help next time if given proper notice."

4. Instead of just saying, "No," you might add, "but thank you for thinking of me."

5. Instead of just saying, "I'm not available," you might add, "but let's talk once my situation changes."

6. Instead of just saying, "I am unable to help with that at this time," you might add, "but is there another way I could help?"

7. Instead of just saying, "I won't be participating," you might add, "but you might ask so-and-so to help."

ENFORCING BOUNDARIES

Simply setting boundaries is often not enough to deter unwanted behaviors. Enforcing boundaries is about your safety and well-being in relationships. You set and enforce

Important: Enforcing boundaries should only be done when safety is not a risk!

boundaries with your words and actions. Be very specific about what you will and will not allow and state the consequences if the other person continues with his or her unwanted actions. By starting with the easy boundaries to set and enforce, you can become more confident before moving on to the more challenging ones. Learning to set and enforce boundaries is a process that will take time. Enlist the help of others whose boundaries you admire.

As you set logical and reasonable consequences for those failing to respect your boundaries, make sure you are willing and able to enforce those consequences. Again, expect to be tested but remain firm.

VIOLATED BOUNDARIES

It is important that you follow through on enforcing your boundaries. If you say you are going to do something, do it.

Let what you say be simply "Yes" or "No"; anything more than this comes from evil. Matthew 5:37 ESV

When someone violates a boundary, there should be consequences. Examples:

1. "If you speed ... I will not allow you to drive."

2. "If you steal ... I will notify the authorities."

3. "If you don't give me advance notice … I won't be able to get what you need in time."

4. "If you come in my room without permission … I will get a lock for my door."

5. "If you text at the dinner table … I will take your phone for the evening."

6. "If you call me names … I will hang up the phone."

7. "You didn't drive here safely … so I will find another ride home."

8. "You didn't clean your room … so you can't go."

9. "If you don't return my car by 6:00 PM … I won't loan it to you again."

10. "If you call during dinnertime … I will not answer your call."

11. "You used my credit card again without permission … so I called the police."

12. "If you talk while I'm trying to work … I will move to another area."

13. "If you tell another dirty joke … I will report you."

14. "If you call me more than once a day … I will not answer you."

15. "If you commit adultery again … I will leave."

16. "You posted my picture on Facebook after I asked you not to … so I unfriended you."

17. "If you continue to pressure me … I will stop answering your calls."

18. "If you come over … I will call the police."

19. "You didn't show up on time … so I left after waiting a few minutes."

20. "If you don't follow the custody order … I will file a report."

ROLE-PLAY 2

The following scenarios offer practice in setting and enforcing boundaries. First, think about the ways you have responded. Then take turns with a partner practicing your new boundaries. Try creating your own responses this time. Again, you may want to prepare by standing tall and appearing confident before speaking. Discuss the activity afterward.

1. **Your daughter assumes you can drop everything you are doing and go pick up her friends to spend the night.**

Past response: _____

_____

New response: _____

_____

2. Your friend often asks to borrow your clothes but seldom returns them.

Past response: _____

_____

New response: _____

_____

3. Your mom wants you to try on clothes you don't like.

Past response: _____

_____

New response: _____

_____

4. Your church calls to ask you to take over an activity because someone else failed to show.

Past response: _____

_____

New response: _____

_____

5. Your unorganized friend has planned a vacation. She calls you late the night before she leaves, asking you to bring her an extra suitcase.

Past response: _____

_____

New response: _____

_____

6. Your co-worker stands closer than you are comfortable.

Past response: _____

_____

New response: _____

_____

7. Your abuser calls to tell you he is going to lower his child support amount.

Past response: _____

_____

New response: _____

_____

At first, it may be quite difficult to say, "No." You may stumble over stating your prepared words. Your heart may race. You may feel guilt or fear of rejection.

Survivor: Having little power in my relationship with my abuser spilled over into my professional life. I had added responsibility at my job, which required me to work closely with a few strong-willed people. In the past, I had avoided confrontations and let others address any problems. However, this time I knew I had to step up as the leader and confront a particular person. As I walked to where she was, my heart was pounding. I felt sick to my stomach, dreading what was to come. I knew how past conflicts with her had gone—not well. As soon as I entered the room, I let her know there was a problem. Without stopping, I took a deep breath and stated the problem, stated what needed to be done to correct it, and stated expectations for future actions. Every time she argued, I restated my position. I didn't back down. In fact, I found myself becoming firmer and my eye contact better with each statement. As I left, I felt a huge rush of adrenalin. I had done it! I felt great! I still have to work at not letting others run over me, but that first victory was a huge step forward.

It's easiest to start setting minor boundaries with people who will support what you are doing. The more you establish boundaries and enforce them, the more empowered you are to follow the path God has for you. Remember, setting boundaries is about what you need to do for yourself to have healthy relationships.

Instead, You direct me on the path that leads to a beautiful life.
As I walk with You, the pleasures are never-ending, and I
know true joy and contentment. Psalm 16:11 VOICE

If the relationship is a healthy one, your boundaries will be respected.

Saying "no" does become easier with practice. When you are ready, make sure you are in a safe environment and move on to setting more difficult boundaries for less agreeable people. Save the most difficult situation and the least agreeable people for last. You may want to ask a supporter to be with you when you set boundaries for the most difficult people. For those who resist your boundaries, you will respectfully set consequences that create some discomfort.

Be prepared for changes in relationships. When we set and enforce boundaries, we risk losing relationships. We risk additional conflict at first as our new boundaries are enforced and challenged. When boundaries are first set and enforced with a child who has been allowed to run wild, the child tends to get worse before they get better. The same is usually true of teenagers and adults. Should you be met with anger, realize those resisting are the ones with character issues, not you. They are the selfish ones wanting the world to revolve around them. They are the ones that avoid responsibility for their actions. They are the ones who feel entitled to have their needs met with no respect for your needs. Plan how you will combat their resistance. Being consistent is an extremely important place to start. If the relationship is a healthy one, your boundaries will be respected. If it is an unhealthy one, the unhealthy roots will be exposed.

> **Survivor**: My daughter wanted a friend to spend the night, but I had already told her I didn't want anyone coming over. However, her little friend insisted she ask me anyway. My daughter said, "She's going to say no." When she asked me, I said, "I already told you tonight is not a good night for company. You know I am not going to change my mind after I've already told you no." My daughter turned to her friend, "See? I told you she would say no. She never changes her mind." Sticking to what I said saved me from a lot of mother-daughter arguments over the years.

It is by consistently enforcing your boundaries that your message becomes clear.

I'm valuable.
My time is valuable.
My gifts and talents are valuable.
My priorities are valuable.
My destiny in Christ is valuable.
I will no longer feel guilty for saying no.
My boundaries will help protect me from fear,
resentment, frustration, and stress.
I will no longer be guilted or coerced into doing
things I am not led to do.
I will help others at the leading of the Holy Spirit.
I will seek God's praise and approval and not that of man.

Brenda Waggoner writes:

As a child of God…
I can choose joy in this life, here and now.

I can choose to relax and have fun, to offer my gifts, dance, sing, make up a recipe, or…

I can choose to say no when I feel something is not safe or I am not ready.

I can choose not to participate in chaotic behavior of family or friends.

I can choose to leave the company of people who lay a guilt trip on me.

I can choose to leave the company of people who manipulate and humiliate me.

I can choose to care for and respect myself. This is not selfish.

I can choose the way I will think and behave and accept all my feelings.

I can feel all my feelings—they are part of me, and God understands.[14]

JOURNAL

Write down a situation where you find it hard to establish a boundary. Which broken record "go-to" phrase would you be comfortable using the next time that situation arises? What consequences will you set? How will you enforce those consequences?

PRAYER

Dear Lord, how wonderful it is to know I can count on You to help me as I deal with others. I know I am not perfect, no one is but Jesus, and I acknowledge my flaws. I want to be the woman You have created me to be, fulfilling the destiny You have for me. I ask for Your help in setting and enforcing boundaries that will allow me to be that woman. Help me to see when others are failing to respect my boundaries, and give me the strength to enforce those boundaries. Help me see when I am violating boundaries so that I can make changes to reflect my respect for others. Give me wisdom, Lord, when I am dealing with difficult, persistent, or abusive people. Let Your joy flood me as I take back my life. In the victorious name of Jesus I pray, Amen.

Lesson 10

FREE TO LOVE

"For I know the plans and thoughts that I have for you,"
says the Lord, "plans for peace and well-being and not for disaster,
to give you a future and a hope." Jeremiah 29:11 AMP

One of the hardest things God asks us to do is forgive those who hurt us. In order to be truly free to enjoy a relationship with Him, God wants us to let go of all the hurt, resentment, anger, and unforgiveness we are holding against Him, our abuser, and even ourselves. He has such great plans for us!

Beloved, I pray that you may prosper in all things and be in health,
just as your soul prospers. 3 John 1:2 NKJV

FORGIVING OUR ABUSER

Survivor: After my marriage ended, I came to realize I was a victim of domestic violence. I never saw the abuse for what it was. As I realized the truth of what had happened to me, I had to deal with the roller coaster of emotions bombarding me, especially the hurt and anger I felt. I had become good at minimizing pain and stuffing most of my emotions—until now. This flood of feelings kept sweeping over me. After months of attending a weekly support group, I accepted my feelings were normal and didn't have to rule my life. Breakthrough, right? That's when a new thought hit me. "I have to forgive him." I didn't want to. With every fiber of my being, I didn't want to forgive him. I wanted him to experience the pain I felt. I wanted him to suffer as I had suffered. As war waged in my head and heart, I finally admitted I had to forgive him, not for his sake but for mine. Holding on to the unforgiveness meant allowing my toxic thoughts to be more important to me than God's Word. I came to realize that not forgiving him gave him the power to keep me from fully enjoying a closer relationship with God. No man is worth that. I made a deliberate choice never to give my abuser or any other person that power. But how was I supposed to forgive someone who had hurt me so terribly for so long? Finally, I asked God to let me see my abuser as He saw him. The picture I got changed my life. You see, the picture I saw was of a worm skewered on a stick, writhing and twisting over an open flame. My compassion rose for that tortured creature. How sad it was that

I didn't want to. With every fiber of my being, I didn't want to forgive him.

his experiences and choices had made him captive to such torment! The Scripture came to me about being turned over to tormenters until what was owed was paid. I knew he could never repay or restore what he had taken from me, but my God could. I chose to forgive. I even found myself asking God to show him mercy and to draw him closer. I prayed God would give him another chance to receive salvation, as his life was in a death spiral. I could now view him as the broken man he was, totally deceived by the enemy and having no peace, no joy, and no hope for a better life because he didn't have a relationship with Jesus. Oh, I still had to continue to forgive him as new memories surfaced in the months to come. But that day, God's heart became my heart.

In one of his letters to the church in Ephesus, Paul wrote, *"Get rid of all bitterness, rage and anger, brawling and slander, along with every form of malice" (Ephesians 4:31 NIV).* Notice the word *all.* It didn't say "some" or "part" or "the ones you want to." God wants *all* the bitterness gone. It's not hard to figure out what we are supposed to do; it's hard to subdue our emotions and let them go when everything in us is yelling, "No way! It's not right! I didn't hurt him; he hurt me!"

The battle that is occurring is between our soul (mind, will, and emotions) and our spirit. The battle is between what you feel and what you know you need to do. Doing the right thing isn't always what makes us feel good at that moment. However, Jesus reminds us in Matthew that if we do not forgive, we are not forgiven.

> *But if you do not forgive others [nurturing your hurt and anger*
> *with the result that it interferes with your relationship with God],*
> *then your Father will not forgive your trespasses. Matthew 6:15 AMP*

> *"Then the master called the servant in. 'You wicked servant,' he said, 'I canceled all that*
> *debt of yours because you begged me to. Shouldn't you have had mercy on your fellow*
> *servant just as I had on you?' In anger his master handed him over to the jailers to be*
> *tortured, until he should pay back all he owed. This is how my heavenly Father will treat*
> *each of you unless you forgive your brother or sister from your heart."*
> *Matthew 18:32-35 NIV*

God sees our heart. Maybe you don't think of yourself in the same category as your abuser—you would never hurt anyone the way you've been hurt—but God doesn't categorize sin as big or small, better or worse. He has not qualified one sin as more egregious than another. To Him, a sin is a sin is a sin.

> *For the word of God is living and active. Sharper than any double-edged sword, it*
> *penetrates even to dividing soul and spirit, joints and marrow; it judges the thoughts and*
> *attitudes of the heart. Nothing in all creation is hidden from God's sight. Everything is*
> *uncovered and laid bare before the eyes of him to whom we must give account.*
> *Hebrews 4:12-13 NIV*

A sin is any thought or action that falls short of God's will and does not reflect His nature and character. God is perfect, and anything we do that falls short of His perfection is sin. That doesn't mean that some sins won't carry heavier consequences on earth, but sin still results in death unless it is confessed and covered by the redemptive blood of Jesus.

> *For all have sinned and fall short of the glory of God. Romans 3:23 NIV*

> *For the wages of sin is death, but the free gift of God [that is, His remarkable,*
> *overwhelming gift of grace to believers] is eternal life in Christ Jesus our Lord.*
> *Romans 6:23 AMP*

The Bible is very clear that harboring bitterness and unforgiveness in our hearts is sin. Unforgiveness complicates and compromises our daily walk with God. If we aren't actively seeking to kill unforgiveness, it will cause a breach in our fellowship with God. We won't experience everything God has to offer us. Part of being in a right relationship with God is allowing Him to be Lord over every area of our life and letting His forgiveness flow over and through us to others. God says it is in our own best interest to forgive, not what is in the best interest of the person who needs to be forgiven. We are the ones God is trying to protect. We are the ones who receive the most benefit from forgiveness, not the other person. Forgiving others spares us from the consequences of living with an unforgiving heart.

And whenever you stand praying, forgive, if you have anything against anyone, so that your Father also who is in heaven may forgive you your trespasses. Mark 11:25 ESV

But I say to you that everyone who is angry with his brother will be liable to judgment. Matthew 5:22 ESV

Survivor: I had a trip to Israel planned for over a year with my mom. I was so excited to be going. The night before I left, my abuser came in from being at the bar and told me he didn't want me and our child to go. Very calmly I told him the plans were made, the money had been paid, and my mom was counting on us to go. I held my breath to see what he would do next. Strangely, he didn't say any more. I should have known better than to believe he would give in so easily.

We had a very early flight to ensure we made our connection with the rest of the group. The next morning, when I tried to wake my abuser to drive us to the airport, he was unresponsive. I tried several times before I realized he was not going to get up and take us. This was his way of letting me know he would get what he wanted, but I wasn't missing this trip! Since I was going to be gone for several days, I had loaned my car to my pastor to take on vacation. I had to call my pastor at 5:00 A.M. to take us to the airport. We missed our flight but were able to get on the next one and still make our connection. I realized God already knew what was going to happen when He impressed on me weeks before to book the earlier of two available flights.

Here I was going on a trip to the Holy Land, and I was so full of anger at my abuser. How dare he try and sabotage such an important, once-in-a-lifetime trip! I wasn't even afraid of his reaction at that point; I was too mad. I refused to let his actions ruin my trip, so I just decided not even to think about him the whole trip and how mad I was. God had other plans, though. We had a wonderful time in Israel. It was truly a deeply emotional, life-changing trip. Toward the end of the itinerary, we visited the site of the Garden Tomb to receive the sacrament of Communion.

Here I am in Israel, at the site believed to be the tomb of Jesus, getting ready to receive Communion. Then I hear the words coming from the pastor leading our trip about searching our hearts to make sure we are right before God. In my head I cried out, "God, You are not playing fair! You know how mad I am! You also know I am not going to pass up an opportunity to have Communion here. God, You are so not playing fair!" With tears streaming down my face, I angrily continued this argument in my mind. I didn't want to think about my abuser. I didn't want to let this offense go. I certainly didn't want to deal with all my anger at such a sacred time. But in the end, as an act of obedience to God, I chose to forgive my abuser for not driving us to the airport. I was able to take Communion.

God knew what He was doing. I could have held onto that unforgiveness for months, but God loved me enough to have me let it go and not become a bitter root that would hinder my relationship with Him. I forgave for my benefit, not my abuser's. It was worth it.

When we hold onto resentment and unforgiveness, we are choosing to relive over and over all the bad things that happened. We are living in a prison of our own making. We risk turning our anger inward and struggling with depression. We are letting our past seep over into our present and affect our future. However, releasing unforgiveness brings us freedom. The choice to forgive comes before the reward of freedom. Being obedient to the Word of God brings love and joy instead of hate and misery.

Therefore if the Son makes you free, you shall be free indeed. John 8:36 NKJV

If you keep My commandments, you will abide in My love, just as I have kept My Father's commandments and abide in His love. These things I have spoken to you, that My joy may remain in you, and that your joy may be full. John 15:10-11 NKJV

- When we forgive someone, we are not endorsing what happened.

- We are not saying what they did was okay.

- We are not saying we agree with what they did or that it was acceptable.

- We are not saying we will continue to permit it.

- What we are saying is that we are not willing to be bitter.

- When we forgive, we are pronouncing that we will insist on living a life of freedom instead of a life full of emotional bondage.

"To forgive someone means to let him off the hook or cancel a debt he owes. When you refuse to forgive someone, you still want something from that person, and even if it is revenge that you want, it keeps you tied to him forever.... It is much better to receive grace from God who has something to give, and to forgive those who have no money to pay the debt with. This ends your suffering because it ends the wish for repayment that is never forthcoming and that makes your heart sick because your hope is deferred (Proverbs 13:12)."[15]

"To forgive means we will never get from that person what was owed us. And that is what we do not like, because that involves grieving for what will never be: the past will not be different."[16]

- We base our forgiveness on our heart attitude, not the actions of those who hurt us. It is not about their repentance but our desire to obey God.

Above all else, guard your heart, for everything you do flows from it. Proverbs 4:23 NIV

- We base our forgiveness on trusting God to take care of justice for us instead of wrongly thinking that we can exact justice better than He can.

Refrain from anger and turn from wrath; do not fret—it leads only to evil. For those who are evil will be destroyed, but those who hope in the Lord will inherit the land.
Psalm 37:8-9

Do not take revenge, my dear friends, but leave room for God's wrath, for it is written: "It is mine to avenge; I will repay," says the Lord. Romans 12:19 NIV

Even though God commands us to forgive others, He never said we are to keep allowing those who hurt us to repeat their actions or to keep trusting those who violated our trust. We are not telling those forgiven, "I'm fine with what you did. Go ahead and abuse me again." We are not denying the reality of the abuse but recognizing abusers rarely have a sincere change of heart. We are not equating forgiveness with reconciliation. We are not interfering with the natural consequences or the accountability for their abusive actions. When we forgive someone, we are stating that we choose

When we forgive, we are declaring we will live life in freedom instead of in emotional bondage.

to release bitterness. When we forgive, we are declaring we will live life in freedom instead of in emotional bondage.

> **Survivor**: There was a time I left for several months. I had discovered he was having an affair with another woman. I was so hurt and angry. After all the times he had accused me, *he* was the one cheating! I remember being in my small apartment kitchen, knowing I had to forgive him because that's what the Word says. With my hands in fists, my teeth clenched, and tears flowing down my face, I remember saying to God, "Fine! You want me to forgive him? Then You're going to have to do it because I can't!" That's exactly what happened. God helped me to forgive in His strength because I couldn't do it in my own. It didn't happen instantaneously. Many times I had to forgive the same hurt over and over, but each time God was there helping me.

Many times I had to forgive the same hurt over and over, but each time God was there helping me.

Forgiveness is a process. The deeper the hurt, the harder it can be to forgive. Sometimes we have to get the feelings out and deal with each incident separately over time. Sometimes new situations arise that require more forgiveness after leaving. Sometimes we think we have forgiven then realize there's more to forgive. That's okay. Each time we forgive, we get a little freer. Avoid condemnation if your journey takes longer than others or longer than you think it should. Condemnation is not of God.

> *There is therefore now no condemnation to them which are in Christ Jesus,*
> *who walk not after the flesh, but after the Spirit. Romans 8:1 KJV*

"FORGIVING" GOD

Both the Book of Psalms and the Book of Job make references to being angry with God.

1. Why is the psalmist upset with God in **Psalm 22:1-2 NLT**? _____

_____

_____.

> *My God, my God, why have you abandoned me? Why are you so far away*
> *when I groan for help? Every day I called you, my God, but you*
> *did not answer. Every night I lift my voice, but I find no relief.*

2. Why is the psalmist upset with God in **Psalm 42:9 NLT**? _____

_____.

> *"O God my rock," I cry, "Why have you forgotten me?*
> *Why must I wander around in grief, oppressed by my enemies?"*

3. Why was David upset with God in **Psalm 35:17 NLT**? _____

_____

_____.

> *How long, O Lord, will you look on and do nothing? Rescue me*
> *from their fierce attacks. Protect my life from these lions!*

4. Why was Job upset with God in **Job 3:23-26 NLT**? _____

_____

_____.

> *Why is life given to those with no future, those God has surrounded*
> *with difficulties? I cannot eat for sighing; my groans pour out like water.*
> *What I always feared has happened to me. What I dreaded has come true.*
> *I have no peace, no quietness. I have no rest; only trouble comes.*

We also get angry with God sometimes, blaming Him for some of the hurtful things that have happened to us. God is big enough to allow us to lash out at Him in our frustration and anger. God is big enough to allow us to "forgive" Him for our sake, not His. God understands He is not guilty. He has done nothing wrong. He is perfect. It is our own misunderstanding and misperceptions that cause us to incorrectly place blame for our pain on God when we are wounded and overwhelmed.

It can be difficult in the midst of troubles to understand why God allows hurtful things to happen to us. We may become angry at Him and yell out our frustration.

> **Survivor**: I left court knowing that once again, my abuser had no consequences. After months of this kind of "justice," I was furious. I pulled into my garage and screamed, "God, where are You? You are supposed to help me! You are the One who is on MY side? Why are You letting him get by with all this? Why is he not held accountable? It's so unfair! He should be punished!" I continued to sob in my car. I wanted answers. I finally left the car to walk inside when I heard God speak to me. He said quietly, "It is not punishment that will change his heart. It is My love." I felt all

that rage drain from my body like a balloon deflating. I knew He was right. His ways are not our ways.

For my thoughts are not your thoughts, neither are your ways my ways, declares the Lord. As the heavens are higher than the earth, so are my ways higher than your ways and my thoughts than your thoughts. Isaiah 55:8–9 NIV

When we are going through trials, it is our choice to run away from God or to run to God. It breaks His heart when we run away and stray from our relationship with Him, choosing other things on which to focus our time and attention. When we run away, we stop reading our Bible, stop praying, stop worshipping with other believers. We withdraw from God and lose track of where He is, even though He is right there with us. We fail to reach out to other believers for support. We become more susceptible to the lies of the enemy, the lies that say, "God doesn't hear you. God doesn't care. God is powerless to help you. God is not real."

It is our choice to run away from God or to run to God.

When we run to God, we find open arms and a place of rest. When we focus our attention on Him, we find comfort and peace. When we draw closer to Him, He draws closer to us, and His love for us keeps the lies of the enemy from having any effect. Holding onto all that anger is exhausting. There is no better place when we are tired and hurting than in His arms.

Come to me, all you who are weary and burdened, and I will give you rest. Matthew 11:28 NIV

I am leaving you with a gift—peace of mind and heart. And the peace I give is a gift the world cannot give. So don't be troubled or afraid. John 14:27 NLT

God reconciled Himself to us through the sacrifice of Christ. Is it a necessity for us to "forgive" God? No. God doesn't need our forgiveness. God always acts righteously despite what our perceptions or misperceptions might be.

Is it necessary for *you* to "forgive" God? Take a hard look at your attitude toward God. Any resentment you hold toward God will not affect Christ, who forgives you, but it will cause you needless emotional pain and grief.

Know that God understands your feelings and thoughts. God is aware of all our deeply felt pain and suffering. The evil in the world breaks God's heart greater than it does ours. It is a powerful image to think that the God who created the universe cares so deeply for us and is so attuned to us that He gently catches every one of our tears and writes down the cause. Those are the actions of our God, who cares about our pain and suffering.

You keep track of all my sorrows. You have collected all my tears in your bottle. You have recorded each one in your book. Psalm 56:8 NLT

I like to use an illustration of a tapestry to help people who are struggling to understand where God is when they are going through trials. Consider we are looking from below at the underside of a tapestry with its untidy, seemingly random threads. It is only when we look from God's point of view, from above, that we can see the beauty of the tapestry with its perfectly designed and executed pattern. What we couldn't see from below now begins to make sense. Trust that the God of all wisdom and knowledge will reveal all hidden things in His timing. The more we know God, the less likely we are to blame Him when bad things happen.

That their hearts might be encouraged, being knit together in love, and attaining to all riches of the full assurance of understanding, to the knowledge of the mystery of God, and of the Father and of Christ, in whom are hidden all the treasures of wisdom and knowledge. Colossians 2:2–3 NKJV

FORGIVING OURSELF

All of us make mistakes. All of us make poor choices. All of us fall short. All of us can be deceived.

Survivor: How could I have been so stupid? How could I let him treat me like that for so long? What was I thinking? Why didn't I just leave? How could I put my child through that? There's no excuse for what I did. Why did I keep going back? How could I believe he loved me when he treated me like that? How could I believe all his lies when everybody else knew the truth? I'm so embarrassed! I'm so ashamed! I'm so mad at myself! How could I have been so stupid?

Do any of those thoughts seem familiar? Just as not forgiving others is harmful, so is not forgiving ourselves. When we don't forgive others, a breeding ground develops for resentment and anger. When we don't forgive ourselves, unforgiveness deepens into shame and guilt and becomes a major source of self-blame. Our harsh thoughts keep circling around and around and around in our head.

I listen to victims encourage one another to be gentle with themselves because the abuse was not their fault. Yet, these same women who are so encouraging to others fail to be gentle with themselves. They feel they are undeserving of forgiveness. They hold themselves to a higher standard than they hold others. Somehow, they are supposed to be smarter, wiser, and more discerning than the rest of us. They are supposed to be above making the same mistakes as other victims. They reject the forgiveness offered by God. Hello, Pride.

> *Pride goes before destruction, and a haughty spirit before a fall.*
> *Proverbs 16:18 ESV*

You cannot go back and change the past. You cannot undo decisions you made. The longer you avoid forgiving yourself, the longer you allow yourself to harbor the feelings that you deserve to suffer for what happened. You are believing the lies of the enemy, not the truth of God's Word. Remember, condemnation is not of God.

There is nothing to gain by holding yourself in unforgiveness; there is everything to gain by releasing yourself from unforgiveness and beginning the process of healing. You can choose to forgive yourself. You can stop punishing yourself and being angry with yourself. You can forgive yourself for letting hurt control you. You can repent and ask for His forgiveness and healing. He loves you and gives you His grace allowing you to move forward. He shows you mercy and offers you His peace.

Survivor: After a decade of having been free, it took a life coach to bring into view the fact that I had yet to let go of the blame I had laid upon myself. I had felt strong, I rebuilt my life, but I couldn't figure out what was holding me back from the full abundance that I knew God had waiting for me. When I realized I had yet to forgive myself, I cried. I let the tears fall, and then I took everything that had ever happened, everything I was still blaming myself for, and I laid it at the feet of Jesus. Freedom, real freedom, and the peace that surpasses all understanding is real. I felt brand new.

Peace I leave with you; my peace I give to you. Not as the world gives do I give to you. Let not your hearts be troubled, neither let them be afraid. John 14:27 ESV

RECEIVING FORGIVENESS FROM GOD

Just as you receive forgiveness for your other sins, you can receive forgiveness for holding onto anger, resentment, and bitterness toward your abuser. Because Jesus died for all your sins, God is willing and able to forgive you.

If we confess our sins, he is faithful and just to forgive us our sins and to cleanse us from all unrighteousness. 1 John 1:9 ESV

For You, Lord, are good, and ready to forgive, and abundant in lovingkindness to all who call upon You. Psalm 86:5 NKJV

He wants you to take all that energy you spend on stoking your unforgiveness and use it to serve Him instead. Search your heart for feelings not only of unforgiveness, anger, bitterness, and resentment but of rejection, betrayal, abandonment, and failure—then release them all. Confess your sin, turn away from your unforgiveness, and set your eyes on the things above.

Set your minds on things above, not on earthly things. Colossians 3:2 NIV

LETTING GO

Forgiving others and ourselves releases us from all those feelings that imprison us and allows us to receive the healing we need. One reason God requires us to forgive is because He does not want anything to stand between Him and us.

God requires us to forgive because He does not want anything to stand between Him and us.

I was once told that holding onto unforgiveness is like drinking poison and expecting the other person to die. The wrong done to you can never be undone. The past will never be different. It's time to take those first steps towards forgiving your abuser, "forgiving" God, and forgiving yourself. It's time to lay the burden of unforgiveness at the foot of the cross.

Casting all your cares [all your anxieties, all your worries, and all your concerns, once and for all] on Him, for He cares about you [with deepest affection, and watches over you very carefully]. 1 Peter 5:7 AMP

Remember who God is. Remember all the times you have been forgiven. Remember how much He loves you and wants His best for you. He wants you to be free from the bondage of unforgiveness. It's time to repent of holding onto unforgiveness one step at a time.

1. Forgiveness starts with purposing in your heart to forgive as an act of obedience. Just say, "I want to forgive."

Blessed are all who fear the Lord, who walk in obedience to him. Psalm 128:1 NIV

Has the Lord as great a delight in burnt offerings and sacrifices as in obedience to the voice of the Lord? Behold, to obey is better than sacrifice, and to heed [is better] than the fat of rams. 1 Samuel 15:22 AMP

2. Admit you are struggling and ask for help. Just say, "I have to forgive but I don't want to. Lord, I need your help."

When he calls to me, I will answer him; I will be with him in trouble; I will rescue him and honor him. Psalm 91:15 ESV

Because He has inclined His ear to me, Therefore I will call upon Him as long as I live. Psalm 116:2 NKJV

Trust in the Lord with all your heart, and lean not on your own understanding. Proverbs 3:5 NKJV

3. Forgive each sin against you. One at a time, name the sin and forgive it. Then name the next sin and forgive it. Continue until all the sins have been named, forgiven, and let go.

> *Create in me a clean heart, O God, and renew a right*
> *spirit within me. Psalm 51:10 ESV*

4. Ask God to forgive you for each sin related to unforgiveness toward Him. Confess each sin against God and seek His forgiveness.

> *I prayed to the Lord my God and confessed: "Lord, the great and awesome God, who*
> *keeps his covenant of love with those who love him and keep his commandments, we*
> *have sinned and done wrong. We have been wicked and have rebelled; we have turned*
> *away from your commands and laws. We have not listened to your servants the*
> *prophets, who spoke in your name to our kings, our princes and our ancestors,*
> *and to all the people of the land." Daniel 9:4-6 NIV*

5. Ask God to show any unforgiveness you have toward yourself. As He reveals each time you have fallen under condemnation, choose to forgive yourself.

> *Then I let it all out; I said, "I'll come clean about my failures to God."*
> *Suddenly the pressure was gone—my guilt dissolved,*
> *my sin disappeared. Psalm 32:5 MSG*

6. Allow God to move you forward on your road to forgiveness. Forgiveness is a heart attitude. It takes time to release and accept His healing for your pain. Don't be swayed by the pressures of well-meaning others who may try to rush you along. A gentle prodding at the leading of the Spirit is one thing; a human push is another. False forgiveness spoken under pressure is not true forgiveness. You can just respond, "I am learning to trust God who is helping me to forgive."

> *Evening and morning and at noon I will pray, and cry aloud,*
> *and He shall hear my voice. Psalm 55:17 KJV*

Begin anew your spiritual journey of intimacy with the Father. Get what you need from God who gives freely. Meditate on His Word, pray, and seek out other believers. Keep your eyes focused on Him.

JOURNAL

Take time to think about and write down what unforgiveness is doing to you physically, emotionally, and spiritually. Consider writing a letter of forgiveness to your abuser. Consider writing another letter of forgiveness to yourself. Write any other letters about which God speaks to you. It is up to you what you choose to do with the letters, but just the act of writing them can be healing.

PRAYER

Loving Father, I am at that place in my healing journey where I am fighting one of my biggest battles and am so grateful I can turn to You for help. I choose to release any unforgiveness that has become a part of me. I have held onto it for so long it has sprouted and grown deep roots. I know that I cannot release all these feelings tied to unforgiveness without Your help. You are the only one powerful enough to help me get rid of unforgiveness toward those who have hurt me. I give You permission to reveal and help me destroy any deep roots of bitterness, anger, resentment, hurt, sense of injustice, shame, guilt, and any other emotions that are not of You. I desire to be free to pursue a full relationship with You with no separation. I want to experience the fullness of joy that comes from being free of the bondage of unforgiveness. Thank you, Father. In the merciful name of Jesus I pray, Amen.

Free to Love Activity

DESTROYING PLATES*

MATERIALS NEEDED:

• 1 plain thrift store plate

• Permanent marker

• Clear plastic bag to enclose the plate

• Safety glasses

• Hammer

DIRECTIONS:

1. Write all the things and people on a plate you are choosing to forgive and let go.

2. Place the plate inside the plastic bag, and place it on the concrete area.

3. Smash your plate with a hammer while wearing safety glasses. Also, for the sake of safety, be careful not to allow the plate to break through the bag.

4. Describe how you felt smashing the plate, symbolizing breaking free and letting go.

This activity will require a hard surface, preferably an outside concrete area.

Lesson 11

THANKSGIVING

Let them give thanks to the Lord for his unfailing love
and his wonderful deeds for mankind. Psalm 107:31 NIV

How can God expect me to have an attitude of gratitude when my life is a mess? Doesn't He know how much turmoil and chaos I have? What is it that I have to be grateful for? Raising three kids on my own? Going back to work after years of being an at-home mom? Driving a clunker car? Living in a house I can't afford because he won't pay child support? Really, God? An attitude of gratitude? I just want to stay in bed and pull the covers up over my head.

Sound familiar? Almost every victim of abuse gets overwhelmed with the changes in her life, and it's hard sometimes to remember any reason for being grateful. However, that is exactly what God says we must do.

In everything give thanks; for this is the will of God in Christ Jesus for you.
1 Thessalonians 5:18 NKJV

Notice it doesn't say "for everything;" it says, "in everything." I would have a hard time thanking God for my abuser hurting me. So how do I match my gratitude to my circumstances? I don't. My thankfulness must stand independent of my circumstances.

When we are going through hard times, our fleshly side wants to whine and complain. We want everyone to suffer right alongside us. We want everyone to know how rough we have it. We're frustrated and angry. Nothing seems to be going our way. I'm not saying that we don't have lots of hard things we are going through, but God always gives us opportunities for thanksgiving. When we focus on everything that is wrong in our lives, nothing seems to get better. Even if we do have a good thing happen, we are so focused on what is not happening we forget to be thankful for what is happening.

> *My thankfulness must stand independent of my circumstances.*

When we do something nice for our kids, we appreciate a thank you. When we do something nice for a friend or co-worker, we enjoy at least a little sign of appreciation. We want to learn to appreciate and be thankful for what He has done. God has the right to expect our gratitude. We want to avoid hearts darkened by ingratitude.

For although they knew God, they did not honor him as God or give thanks to him, but they became futile in their thinking, and their foolish hearts were darkened.
Romans 1:21 ESV

The more we get to a place in our lives where we are truly grateful for every moment, every challenge, and every blessing, large and small, the more we can focus on the goodness of God.

Oh give thanks to the Lord, for he is good, for his steadfast love endures forever! Let the redeemed of the Lord say so, whom he has redeemed from trouble. Psalm 107:1-2 ESV

Oh, taste and see that the Lord is good! Blessed is the man who takes refuge in him! Psalm 34:8 ESV

How great is your goodness that you have stored up for those who fear you, that you have given to those who trust you. You do this for all to see. Psalm 31:19 NCV

Every good and perfect gift is from above, coming down from the Father of the heavenly lights, who does not change like shifting shadows. James 1:17 NIV

The more we focus on our problems or the lack of justice in our lives, the more we are falling into the enemy's trap.

Be sober, be vigilant; because your adversary the devil walks about
like a roaring lion, seeking whom he may devour. 1 Peter 5:8 NKJV

The thief does not come except to steal, and to kill, and to destroy.
I have come that they may have life, and that they may have
it more abundantly. John 10:10 NKJV

Jesus operated in thanksgiving. Even before the multiplication of the fish and loaves, Jesus thanked God ahead of time for what He was going to do. Even before He raised Lazarus from the dead, Jesus thanked God for what had already happened. He spoke His thanksgiving aloud so others could hear Him thanking and praising God. When we are buried inside of pain, we need to remember to thank God, in advance, for what we know He can do.

And Jesus took the loaves, and when He had given thanks He distributed them to the
disciples, and the disciples to those sitting down; and likewise of the fish,
as much as they wanted. John 6:11 NKJV

Jesus said to her, "Did I not say to you that if you would believe you would see the glory
of God?" Then they took away the stone from the place where the dead man was lying.
And Jesus lifted up His eyes and said, "Father, I thank You that You have heard Me. And
I know that You always hear Me, but because of the people who are standing by I said
this, that they may believe that You sent Me." Now when He had said these things, He
cried with a loud voice, "Lazarus, come forth!" And he who had died came out bound
hand and foot with graveclothes, and his face was wrapped with a cloth. Jesus said to
them, "Loose him, and let him go." John 11:40-44 NKJV

You may have noticed that thanksgiving and praise are interconnected. Have you noticed the presence of God accompanies thanksgiving and praise? And after we pass through His gates with thanksgiving and into His courts with praise, we can then enter into His very presence.

Come, let us sing to the Lord! Let us shout joyfully to the Rock of our salvation. Let us come to him with thanksgiving. Let us sing psalms of praise to him. Psalm 95:1-2 NLT

*Enter into His gates with thanksgiving, and into His courts with praise.
Be thankful to Him, and bless His name. For the Lord is good; His mercy is everlasting, and His truth endures to all generations. Psalm 100:4-5 NKJV*

*They shall eagerly utter the memory of Your abundant goodness
and will shout joyfully of Your righteousness. Psalm 145:7 NASB*

*And the Levites who were musicians—Asaph, Heman, Jeduthun, and all their sons and brothers—were dressed in fine linen robes and stood at the east side of the altar playing cymbals, lyres, and harps. They were joined by 120 priests who were playing trumpets. The trumpeters and singers performed together in unison to praise and give thanks to the Lord. Accompanied by trumpets, cymbals, and other instruments, they raised their voices and praised the Lord with these words: "He is good! His faithful love endures forever!" At that moment a thick cloud filled the Temple of the Lord.
2 Chronicles 5:12-13 NLT*

God wants us to get to a place where we live a life of gratitude. I once was told a story about two dogs. The one that was fed grew. The one that was not fed did not grow. It is the same with our thoughts. If we focus on thoughts of gratitude, those thoughts will grow. If we focus on thoughts of ingratitude, those thoughts will grow.

REASONS TO BE THANKFUL

*Finally, brethren, whatever things are true, whatever things are noble,
whatever things are just, whatever things are pure, whatever things are lovely,
whatever things are of good report, if there is any virtue and if there is anything
praiseworthy—meditate on these things. Philippians 4:8 NKJV*

1. If you are having trouble finding reasons to be thankful, you can be thankful that you are breathing. That may sound ridiculous; however, your breath is not guaranteed. It is a gift from God. We are not entitled to it, yet we take for granted that we will continue breathing. If it is hard to bear where you are right now, then you may need to break down your gratitude minute by minute. So many times, our lives may have

been threatened, yet here we are—alive. Not all victims are so blessed. That can be your first reason to be grateful. Thank You, God, for _____.

Thus says God the Lord, Who created the heavens and
stretched them out, who spread forth the earth and that which
comes from it, who gives breath to the people on it,
and spirit to those who walk on it. Isaiah 42:5 NKJV

2. Here's another reason to be thankful. If you are attending this study in a group, someone cared enough to include you. Thank You, God, for _____ _____.

Therefore encourage one another and build each other up,
just as in fact you are doing. 1 Thessalonians 5:11 NIV

3. You can be thankful that God is who He is. Thank You, God, that are You are _____ _____ _____ _____.

"I am the Alpha and the Omega," says the Lord God, "who is, and who was,
and who is to come, the Almighty." Revelation 1:8 NIV

They will wage war against the Lamb, but the Lamb will triumph over them
because he is Lord of lords and King of kings . . .Revelation 17:14 NIV

For to us a child is born, to us a son is given; and the government shall be upon his
shoulder, and his name shall be called Wonderful Counselor, Mighty God,
Everlasting Father, Prince of Peace. Isaiah 9:6 ESV

4. You can be grateful for His sacrifice. Thank You, Jesus, for _____ _____ _____.

Through the Son, then, God decided to bring the whole universe back to himself. God
made peace through his Son's blood on the cross and so brought back to himself all
things both on earth and in heaven. At one time you were far away from God and were
his enemies because of the evil things you did and thought. But now, by means of the

physical death of his Son, God has made you his friends, in order to bring you, holy, pure, and faultless, into his presence. Colossians 1:20-22 GNB

Christ hath redeemed us from the curse of the law, being made the curse for us. Galatians 3:13 KJV

But he endured the suffering that should have been ours, the pain that we should have borne. All the while we thought that his suffering was punishment sent by God. But because of our sins he was wounded, beaten because of the evil we did. We are healed by the punishment he suffered, made whole by the blows he received. All of us were like sheep that were lost, each of us going his own way. But the LORD made the punishment fall on him, the punishment all of us deserved. Isaiah 53:4-6 GNB

5. You can be grateful for what He is going to do. Thank You, God, for _____

_____

_____

_____.

"For I know the plans I have for you," says the Lord, "plans for well-being and not for trouble, to give you a future and a hope. Then you will call upon Me and come and pray to Me, and I will listen to you." Jeremiah 29:11-12 NLT

Survivor: A couple of years after leaving my abuser, I was talking to God. "God, it's really crazy how little ol' me from (City), (State) ended up here in Podunk, (State)." God answered back, "It is no accident you are here. I knew the job you would need to have. I knew the church family you would need to have. I knew the car you would need to have. (I had bought a new car two months before my marriage fell apart.) I knew the friends you would need to have. It is no accident you are here. I had already been to your tomorrow, and I knew what you would need." Wow! That conversation with God changed my life. God has already been to our tomorrow and knows what we will need!

God has already been to our tomorrow.

AN ATTITUDE OF GRATITUDE

Once we start focusing on being grateful, it becomes easier to display an attitude of gratitude by remembering the things God has done for us, recognizing the things He is doing, and having faith in what He is going to do. Thank God continuously throughout the day for the small blessings and the big ones.

Here are some examples of declarations of gratitude that we can make.

1. I thank You, God, that I belong to You.

2. I thank You, God, that I can give my cares to You.

3. I thank You, God, I have gas in my car.

4. I thank You, God, my children are healthy.

5. I thank You, God, we have a safe place to stay.

6. I thank You, God, we have food in our bellies.

7. I thank You, God, that my bills are paid.

8. I thank You, God, that You have that perfect job for me.

9. I thank You, God, my boss sees my value.

10. I thank You, God, that You never leave me.

QUESTIONS:

1. Take a few moments and ask God to remind you of things in the past He has done for you. Write down what came to mind. _____
_____
_____
_____

2. Now ask God to show you what He is doing for you right now. Write down what you heard. _____
_____
_____
_____

3. Last, ask God to show you the things He wants to do for you in the future. Write them down. _____

_____

_____

_____

MAKING DECLARATIONS

Another way of developing a heart of gratitude is by thanking God for His promises in the form of a declaration. When we thank God for answers found in His word, we give Him glory. Saying our declarations aloud helps to build our faith.

Instead of speaking to God about my circumstances, I speak to my circumstances the Word of God.

For all the promises of God find their Yes in him. That is why it is through him that we utter our Amen to God for his glory. 2 Corinthians 1:20 ESV

So then faith comes by hearing, and hearing by the word of God. Romans 10:17 NKJV

1. I thank You, God, that you make me the head and not the tail. (Deuteronomy 28:13)

2. I thank You, God, I am more than a conqueror through You who made me. (Romans 8:37)

3. I thank You, God, I am fearfully and wonderfully made. (Psalm 139:14)

4. I thank You, God, that I win favor with God and man. (Proverbs 3:4)

5. I thank You, God, I can do all things through Christ who strengthens me. (Philippians 4:13)

6. I thank You, God, You have not given me a spirit of fear but of power, and of love, and of a sound mind. (2 Timothy 1:7)

Giving thanks keeps our eyes off our problems and on His promises. I love declarations. They stir me to faith. They build my confidence in God (one evangelist calls it "Godfidence"). They create a sense of expectancy. That's when I get bold. Instead of speaking to God about my circumstances, I speak to my circumstances the Word of God. Hallelujah!

QUESTIONS

What other declarations can you make based on the Word?

1. *Train up a child in the way he should go, and when he is old he will not depart from it. Proverbs 22:6 NKJV* _____

_____

2. *When my father and my mother forsake me, then the Lord will take care of me. Psalm 27:10 NKJV* _____

_____

3. *Come to Me, all you who labor and are heavy laden, and I will give you rest. Matthew 11:28 NKJV* _____

_____

4. *A faithful man will abound with blessing. Proverbs 28:20 NKJV* _____

_____

5. *When a man's ways please the Lord, He makes even his enemies to be at peace with him. Proverbs 16:7 NKJV* _____

_____

TURNING SCRIPTURES INTO DECLARATIONS

Let's look at these Scriptures.

[1] O Lord, deliver me from evil men. Preserve me from the violent, [2] who plot and stir up trouble all day long. [3] Their words sting like poisonous snakes. [4] Keep me out of their power. Preserve me from their violence, for they are plotting against me.
Psalm 140:1-4 TLB

[6] Do not worry about anything, but pray and ask God for everything you need, always giving thanks. [7] And God's peace, which is so great we cannot understand it, will keep your hearts and minds in Christ Jesus. Philippians 4:6-7 NCV

[10] So that you will live the kind of life that honors and pleases the Lord in every way. You will produce fruit in every good work and grow in the knowledge of God. [11] God

will strengthen you with his own great power so that you will not give up when troubles come, but you will be patient. Colossians 1:10-11 NCV

We can turn these same Scriptures into declarations of gratitude.

¹O Lord, deliver me from evil men. Preserve me from the violent, ²who plot and stir up trouble all day long. Thank You, O Lord, for delivering me from evil men. Thank You for preserving me from the violent who plot and stir up trouble all day long. *³Their words sting like poisonous snakes. ⁴Keep me out of their power. Preserve me from their violence, for they are plotting against me.* I thank You, Jesus, that although their words sting like poisonous snakes, You keep me out of their power. Thank You for preserving me from their violence as they plot against me.

⁶Do not worry about anything, but pray and ask God for everything you need, always giving thanks. ⁷And God's peace, which is so great we cannot understand it, will keep your hearts and minds in Christ Jesus. Thank You, God, that I don't have to worry about anything. Thank You for giving me everything I need. I thank You for Your peace that is so great I can't even understand it but keeps my heart and mind focused on You, Jesus.

¹⁰So that you will live the kind of life that honors and pleases the Lord in every way. You will produce fruit in every good work and grow in the knowledge of God. ¹¹God will strengthen you with his own great power so that you will not give up when troubles come, but you will be patient. I want to thank You that I can live a life that honors and pleases You in every way. I will produce good fruit in every good work I do and grow in Your knowledge. You will strengthen me with Your own great power so that I will not give up when trouble comes but will be patient.

Can you sense your heart attitude changing and your faith increasing? See if you can turn these Scriptures into declarations.

You will keep him in perfect peace, whose mind is stayed on You, because he trusts in You. Isaiah 26:3 NKJV _____

_____

_____

But those who wait on the Lord Shall renew their strength; They shall mount up with wings like eagles, They shall run and not be weary, They shall walk and not faint. Isaiah 40:31 NKJV _____

_____

_____

_____

PERSONALIZING SCRIPTURES

Another thing we can do is personalize Scripture by inserting our name as if God is speaking directly to us—because He is! What an awesome reason to be thankful! Below is Psalm 91 NKJV. Insert your name in the blank and make it personal.

¹_____ *who dwells in the secret place of the Most High shall abide under the shadow of the Almighty.* ²_____ *will say of the Lord, "He is my refuge and my fortress; My God, in Him I will trust."* ³*Surely He shall deliver* _____ *from the snare of the fowler and from the perilous pestilence.* ⁴*He shall cover* _____ *with His feathers, and under His wings* _____ *shall take refuge; His truth shall be* _____ *shield and buckler.* ⁵_____ *shall not be afraid of the terror by night, nor of the arrow that flies by day,* ⁶*Nor of the pestilence that walks in darkness, nor of the destruction that lays waste at noonday.* ⁷*A thousand may fall at* _____*'s side, and ten thousand at* _____*'s right hand; but it shall not come near her.* ⁸*Only with* _____*s eyes shall she look, and see the reward of the wicked.* ⁹*Because* _____ *has made the Lord, who is* _____*'s refuge, even the Most High,* _____*'s dwelling place,* ¹⁰*No evil shall befall* _____, *nor shall any plague come near* _____*s dwelling;* ¹¹*For He shall give His angels charge over* _____, *to keep* _____ *in all her ways.* ¹²*In their hands they shall bear* _____ *up, lest she dashes her foot against a stone.* ¹³_____ *shall tread upon the lion and the cobra, the young lion and the serpent* _____ *shall trample underfoot.* ¹⁴*"Because* _____ *has set her love upon Me, therefore I will deliver her; I will set* _____ *on high, because* _____ *has known My name.* ¹⁵_____ *shall call upon Me, and I will*

answer her; I will be with _____ *in trouble; I will deliver* _____ *and honor* _____. *¹⁶With long life I will satisfy* _____, *and show her My salvation.*

What a powerful psalm to let us know that God is looking out for us! What powerful reasons to offer Him thanksgiving! We need to understand that we serve a good God who only wants the best for us. We need to believe that His best for us *is* the best for us.

Additional Scriptures to personalize:

Therefore I also, after I heard of _____*'s faith in the Lord Jesus and* _____*'s love for all the saints, do not cease to give thanks for* _____, *making mention of* _____ *in my prayers: that the God of our Lord Jesus Christ, the Father of glory, may give to* _____ *the spirit of wisdom and revelation in the knowledge of Him, the eyes of* _____*'s understanding being enlightened; that* _____ *may know what is the hope of His calling, what are the riches of the glory of His inheritance in the saints, and what is the exceeding greatness of His power toward us who believe, according to the working of His mighty power which He worked in Christ when He raised Him from the dead and seated Him at His right hand in the heavenly places. Ephesians 1:15-20 NKJV*

For this reason I bow my knees to the Father of our Lord Jesus Christ, from whom the whole family in heaven and earth is named, that He would grant _____, *according to the riches of His glory, to be strengthened with might through His Spirit in the inner man, that Christ may dwell in* _____*'s hearts through faith; that* _____, *being rooted and grounded in love, may be able to comprehend with all the saints what is the width and length and depth and height—to know the love of Christ which passes knowledge; that* _____ *may be filled with all the fullness of God. Ephesians 3:14-19 NKJV*

THANKSGIVING NO MATTER WHAT

Sometimes the things happening don't make sense until we can look back later and see God's hand working behind the scenes. We learn to have faith that God is working on our behalf, even if we don't see it. We come to understand there is a reason to be thankful, even during our storms when we can't see what God is doing.

- A lady was frustrated that court was postponed again. Days later, she found out she needed surgery; her abuser paid for her insurance. Had court been held on the original date, she wouldn't have had insurance, so all medical expenses would have been her responsibility.

- A lady was aggravated that her case was taking months longer than expected. In the interim, the joint assets greatly appreciated in value, so her share got a lot bigger.

- A lady was disheartened her case was taking so long. Over time, she came to realize God was revealing hidden assets of her abuser amounting to tens of thousands of dollars.

Let us be perpetual praisers and not chronic complainers.

Survivor: I was driving back from visiting friends when I got pulled over. I was aggravated to get that ticket even though I was speeding. It was funny how efficient that officer was. I was back on the road in less than five minutes. A couple of miles later, traffic on the highway was at a standstill. It seems a tanker truck had overturned on the bridge. Other vehicles were involved. By calculating the distance and time, I realized that ticket I got kept me from being in the midst of that accident. God was working on my behalf behind the scenes even when I couldn't see it. In addition, I had purchased a box of oranges to support the church youth fundraiser before I left. While we were stuck on the highway for hours, I was able to offer oranges to families with children who were crying because they were hungry and thirsty. God is so good!

The rewards of having a grateful heart are immense. Let us repent of focusing on our lack instead of being grateful for every good thing. Let us focus on the goodness of God instead of letting the attacks of the enemy steal our joy. Let us be perpetual praisers and not chronic complainers. In everything, give thanks.

Always giving thanks to God the Father for everything,
in the name of our Lord Jesus Christ. Ephesians 5:20 NIV

JOURNAL

Write down the challenges you're having right now. Find corresponding Scriptures that state what God says about each one, and write them down. Read the Scriptures aloud often, and thank Him for His Word.

PRAYER

Abba Father, thank You for helping me see Your goodness when my eyes are so clouded with the things of this world. I repent, Father, for taking Your goodness, kindness, and mercy for granted. Help me cultivate an attitude of gratitude. Help me always be grateful for who You are, what You have done, and what You are going to do in my life. Help me speak to my circumstances about You instead of speaking to You about my circumstances. Help me to build my faith by speaking aloud Your Word. Help me believe Your promises. Let my heart be overwhelmed by all Your blessings. In the awesome name of Jesus I pray, Amen.

Thanksgiving Activity

STICKY NOTES

MATERIALS NEEDED:

- 1 pad of 2x2 sticky notes
- Writing utensil

DIRECTIONS:

1. Write different things for which you are thankful on about a third of the sticky notes.

2. Now write different declarations regarding what God says about difficult circumstances you are experiencing on another third of the sticky notes.

3. On the last third of the sticky notes, write Scriptures personalized with your name.

4. Place these sticky notes around your home (mirrors and inside cabinet doors are favorite places), workplace, and vehicle as reminders to maintain an attitude of thankfulness.

I am thankful my children are healthy.

I can cast my cares on Him because He cares for me.
1 Peter 5:7

For God has not given Char a spirit of fear but of power and of love and of a sound mind.
2 Tim 1:7

Lesson 12

BECOMING A CHILD OF GOD

See what great love the Father has lavished on us, that we should be called children of God! And that is what we are! The reason the world does not know us is that it did not know him. 1 John 3:1 NIV

Survivor: The two greatest gifts my parents gave me were raising me in church and encouraging me in music. The two greatest gifts my abuser gave me were my daughter and my faith. I'm not saying it was God's will for me to be abused, but out of that abuse, I became a woman of prayer and of faith. What the devil meant for evil, God used for good.

I don't remember ever not going to church as a child. My dad was a respected leader, a Sunday School teacher, and a godly man. My mother was always serving. I was active in the youth groups at school and church. I had a serious God encounter at a summer youth camp and was baptized at age 13. Then I went off to college—and left God at home. I had a relationship for several years that ended painfully. As I continued to drift farther away from my church family and all things related to God, I began to question if He was even real. My friends were not Christians, so there was no one to encourage me in my faith. Sleeping in on the weekends seemed more important than church.

My next relationship was far from a godly one. I was making a lot of choices that were definitely outside His will that cost me dearly. When that relationship ended badly, I decided to move back to my hometown. I knew my parents would expect me to attend church, so I started getting involved again. However, I was not as grounded in my faith as I am now. I didn't have that personal relationship with Jesus yet that would shape the woman I was to become. I knew about Jesus, but I didn't know Jesus.

I married my abuser still damaged from my previous relationships and still apart from God. It was after a particularly intense spewing of his hateful words that I slid down to the floor and cried out to God for help. Despite me being far from God, He was not far from me. I distinctly remember feeling a wave of warmth flow over me from my head to my toes. I knew it was God. God had heard me! I got out the phone book (pre-internet!) and picked a church to attend on Sunday. As God would have it, I ended up at a different church than the one I had picked out. The two churches were close together, and I went in the first one I saw. However, it was definitely the right church for me. The people were so welcoming and plugged me into a small group within the first few weeks. Smart choice. I was so hungry for God and to learn what His Word said. Within months, we moved away from that church. I commuted for a while but was pregnant, and my pregnancy was not an easy one.

Had it not been for God, I believe I would be dead.

Through a series of people and events, I eventually ended up at the church that really helped me grow and mature as a Christian. This pastor understood my hunger for God and patiently answered all my questions. Under his leadership, I came to know and receive the love, grace, and mercy of God. I came to know about spiritual authority and the spirit realm. I came to understand how the Word of God is living and sustains me. I experienced the power of faith, the power of prayer, and the power of His Word on countless occasions. I saw the gifts of the Spirit (1 Corinthians 12) operate as I associated with Christians who displayed the fruit of the Spirit (Galatians 5) every day. I learned how to pray privately and publicly, how to study and apply the Scriptures to my life, and how to worship in spirit and truth. I learned how to live in hope and victory. I learned how to allow God to be my strength and my refuge, my peace and my rest. I learned how to be still and listen for the voice of God. I was exposed to some of the greatest teachers and teachings available today. I use that knowledge now to encourage and disciple others in their walk with Christ, especially the broken and the hurting. Had it not been for God, I believe I would be dead. I owe Him my life.

Just as God drew me to a personal, saving relationship with Him, He wants to draw you into a personal relationship with Him, too. God loves you. He wants to have a relationship with you through His Son, Jesus Christ. We were created so God could have fellowship with us and for us to have fellowship with God. How awesome is that? The Creator of the entire universe wants you and me! He doesn't need us; He wants us.

The only thing separating you from God is sin. It's the same sin that separated me from God. Sin is simply our inability to be perfect and not break any of God's laws. Only Jesus is perfect; only Jesus is without sin, and God understands that. We sin through our actions, inactions, choices, attitudes, and thoughts. No matter how hard we try or how good we try to be, we can't meet God's standards for righteousness. We are all sinners, and sin separates us from God.

For all have sinned and fall short of the glory of God. Romans 3:23 NIV

If we can't be good enough, what do we do? For us to become a child of God, we can't just clean ourselves up; we have to get rid of our sin problem. For us to become a child of God, the punishment for our sin must be paid. Because He loves us so much, God sent His only Son, Jesus, as a gift to us to save us.

For God so loved the world that he gave his one and only Son, that whoever believes in him shall not perish, but have eternal life. For God did not send his Son into the world to condemn the world, but to save the world through him. John 3:16-17 NIV

Jesus paid the debt and provided salvation for each of us when He sacrificed His life by being crucified on the cross at Calvary. He paid for each of us to have eternal life in Heaven with Him.

For the wages of sin is death, but the gift of God is eternal life
in Jesus Christ our Lord. Romans 6:23 NIV

He saved us, not because of righteous things we had done,
but because of his mercy. Titus 3:5 NIV

We can't get rid of this sin debt on our own, so Jesus paid the debt for us. Yes, He loves us that much!

But God demonstrates His own love for us in this: While we
were still sinners, Christ died for us. Romans 5:8 NIV

It is God's gift of grace that allows us to come to Him, not our own efforts to be a good person or work our way into God's favor to get into Heaven. We can't buy it; we can't earn it. Yes, grace is a free gift for us, but it cost Jesus His very life. It is up to each of us to accept His gift.

For it is by grace you have been saved, through faith—and this is not from yourselves, it is the gift of God—not by works, so that no one can boast. Ephesians 2:8-9 NIV

When we realize how much our sin grieves God and how desperately we need a Savior to reconcile us to right relationship with Him, we are drawn by the Holy Spirit to accept God's offer of salvation. He provided the only way for us to have a personal relationship with Him—through Jesus, who God raised from the dead.

So, what do you have to do to receive salvation through the sacrifice of Jesus Christ and become His child?

1. Admit you are a sinner in need of a Savior.

2. Ask forgiveness for your sins.

3. Believe in your heart that Jesus, God's only Son, died and paid the full debt for your sins.

4. Believe God raised Jesus from the dead to make you a new creation.

5. Confess Jesus as your Lord, and ask Him to be in control of your life.

6. Receive Him as your Savior now and forever.

If you declare with your mouth, "Jesus is Lord," and believe in your heart that God raised him from the dead, you will be saved. For it is with your heart that you believe and are justified, and it is with your mouth that you profess your faith and are saved. Romans 10:9-10 NIV

God says that if we believe in His Son, Jesus, we can live our best life forever with Him in Heaven. But what about now? Now we are adopted into His family with all the rights and privileges of children of God. Hallelujah!

But as many as received Him, to them He gave the right to become children of God, even to those who believe in His name. John 1:12 NASB

In the same way, I tell you, joy breaks out in the presence of God's angels over one sinner who changes both heart and life. Luke 15:10 CEB

JOURNAL

Discuss what this Scripture means to you: *"I will be a Father to you, And you shall be My sons and daughters, says the Lord Almighty." 2 Corinthians 6:18 NKJV.*

SUGGESTED PRAYER

Merciful Father, I know that I am a sinner. I know that I have broken your laws and that my sins have separated me from You. I am truly sorry for the life I have lived and ask for Your forgiveness for my sins. Please help me avoid sinning again. I believe in my heart that Your only Son, Jesus Christ, died for my sins at the cross of Calvary, was raised from the dead, and is alive. I now wish to follow Jesus as my Lord and as my Savior. I invite Jesus to take control of my life and to rule and reign in my heart. I invite Your Holy Spirit to help me obey You and to teach me Your ways. Help me bring glory to You. Thank You, Jesus, for dying for me and giving me eternal life with You in Heaven. Thank You for blessing me as Your child each day here on earth. Thank You for Your gift of grace. I can't wait to experience the fullness of Your love. In the glorious name of Jesus I pray, Amen.

Closing

FINAL THOUGHTS

Congratulations! You made it through all the lessons! I know it may not have always been easy. It wasn't for me either. *I'm Not That Woman Anymore: A Journey to Healing from Abuse* reflects the lessons I needed to learn during my own journey to healing. My journey has been long, difficult, and fraught with emotions. Still, I took the time I needed to embrace the woman I am now as I continue on the journey to being the woman God destined me to be.

Although some of these past weeks may have been challenging, I trust you count the time as well spent. While confronting the lies of the enemy can be exhausting, the freedom that comes when we truly see the Father's heart for His daughters is life-changing. It is my prayer that the lessons in this Bible study have brought you to a place of truth, freedom, healing, and hope. I sincerely desire that you can honestly now say, "I'm not that woman anymore," as an indicator of what has occurred during this Bible study through the power of God's word and the working of the Holy Spirit in you.

PRAYER

The Lord bless you, and keep you [protect you,
sustain you, and guard you];

The Lord make His face shine upon you [with favor],

And be gracious to you [surrounding you with lovingkindness];

The Lord lift up His countenance (face) upon you
[with divine approval],

And give you peace [a tranquil heart and life].
Numbers 6:24-26 AMP

In the precious name of Jesus I pray, Amen.

NEVERTHELESS

Day after day, night after night
I cry out to You, but I can't hear You
My soul is weeping; my heart is breaking
I'm searching for You, but I can't find You

Nevertheless, nevertheless, I know You're here
And Your heart is breaking, too
Nevertheless, nevertheless, You hold me in Your arms
I will make it through because of You

This crushing weight; I'm growing weak
I cry out to You, but I can't hear You
My pain surrounds me; darkness closes in
I'm searching for You, but I can't find You

Nevertheless, nevertheless, I know You're here
And Your heart is breaking, too
Nevertheless, nevertheless, You hold me in Your arms
I will make it through because of You

I will praise You in the midst of my pain
I will praise You in the middle of my storm
I will praise you when the enemy tries to take me out
But he can't
Because You're with me, and I belong to You

You are my strength; You are my hope
You are my help in times of trouble
You're my strong tower; my place of refuge
And I can rest under Your wing

I will praise You in the midst of my pain
I will praise You in the middle of my storm
I will praise you when the enemy tries to take me out
But he can't

I have the victory
I have the victory
I have the victory

Written by Dr. Char Newbold

ENDNOTES

1 Father Heart Communications at their website: https://www.fathersloveletter.com. Please feel free to copy and share with others.

2 Marie M. Fortune. *Keeping the Faith.* (San Francisco, CA: Harper Collins Publishers, Inc., 1987), 15.

3 J.A. Macdonald. Bible Hub, "Retaliation" at their website: https://biblehub.com/sermons/auth/macdonald/retaliation.htm.

4 Tim Keller. *Counterfeit Gods: Empty Promises of Money, Sex, and Power, and the Only Hope that Matters.* (New York: Penguin, 2009), xvii.

5 James MacDonald. *Thinking Differently: Nothing Is Different Until You Think Differently.* (Nashville, TN: LifeWay Press, 2016), 114-116.

6 Douglas Noll. *De-escalate: How to Calm an Angry Person in 90 Seconds or Less.* (New York, NY: Atria Paperback, 2017), 45.

7 Dr. Caroline Leaf. *Who Switched Off My Brain? Controlling Toxic Thoughts and Emotions.* (Inprov, 2009), 15-18.

8 MacDonald, 138.

9 Don Gossett. *What You Say Is What You Get.* (New Kensington, PA: Whitaker House, 1976), 15-16.

10 Billy Graham. *Hope for the Troubled Heart: Finding God in the Midst of Pain.* (New York: Bantam e-book, 1990), 181-193.

11 John Paul Jackson. *I AM: 365 Names of God.* (Streams Publications, 2002), vii and ix.

12 Adapted from Center for Disease Control and Prevention National Center for Injury Prevention. *Choose Respect Community Action Kit: Helping Preteens and Teens Build Healthy Relationships.* (2005).

13 Dr. Henry Cloud and Dr. John Townsend. *Boundaries: When to Say Yes When to Say No to Take Control of Your Life.* (Grand Rapids, MI: Zondervan, 1992), 105-120.

14 Brenda Waggoner. *The Myth of the Submissive Christian Woman: Walking with God without Being Stepped on by Others.* (Wheaton, IL: Tyndale House Publishers, Inc, 2004), 35.

15 Cloud and Townsend, 134-135.

16 Ibid, 263.

Resources

1. Relationship Red Flags

2. Starting a New Relationship

3. Relationship Rights

4. Creating Healthy Boundaries

5. Setting Boundaries: Go-To Statements

6. Controlling Relationship Assessment at https://www.guilford.com/add/forms/fontes3.pdf

7 Hurt by Love at https://www.hurtbylove.com/what-is-abuse-3/abuse-assessment/

8. Cycle of Violence at https://domesticviolence.org/cycle-of-violence/

9. The Duluth Model Wheels at https://www.theduluthmodel.org/wheels/

10. Safety Planning

11. Path to Safety at https://www.thehotline.org/create-a-safety-plan/

12. Additional Websites:
    - Faith Trust Institute at https://faithtrustinstitute.org/resources/learn-the-basics
    - Focus Ministries at www.focusministries1.org/resources
    - DomesticShelters.org at www.domesticshelters.org
    - National Domestic Violence Hotline and 24-Hour Chatline at www.thehotline.org/
    - National Domestic Violence Resources at www.thehotline.org/resources
    - National Coalition Against Domestic Violence at https://ncadv.org

RELATIONSHIP RED FLAGS

Red flags are the warning signs that the person you are in a relationship with, or are contemplating a relationship with, may be potentially abusive. A few signs can show there is potential for abuse. The more signs a person possesses, the more likely the person is abusive.

1. Is overly involved in partner's daily life

2. Desires to "fast track" the relationship

3. Presents as rescuer/protector

4. Expresses strong opinions/beliefs

5. Violates individual rights and boundaries

6. Makes all decisions

7. Monitors partner's whereabouts, activities, spending

8. Displays extreme jealousy/possessiveness

9. Makes unfounded accusations

10. Has bitterness/unresolved past relationship issues

11. Has history of stalking

12. Has history of trouble with law enforcement/fighting

13. Exhibits explosive temper

14. Makes threats of violence

15. Displays hypersensitivity/overreactions

16. Minimizes/disregards partner's feelings/opinions

17. Dismisses partner's problems/concerns/needs as irritational/unimportant

18. Has poor family/friend relationships

19. Isolates partner from others

20. Is self-centered

21. Exhibits immaturity/emotional insecurity/dependency

22. Displays most emotions as anger; difficulty conveying other emotions

23. Has false sense of superiority masking low self-esteem

24. Feels entitled to treat others as inferior

25. Becomes angry if wishes are not anticipated and fulfilled

26. Makes constant putdowns/belittling comments

27. Has frequent anger/hostility toward someone/something

28. Has extreme personality changes (Jekyll/Hyde)

29. Behaves very differently around others than when alone with partner

30. Is unable to communicate in a healthy way

31. Is closed to criticism or suggestions

32. Uses force during arguments

33. Expects advice/orders to be followed

34. Has unspoken/ever-changing rules

35. Expects unwavering loyalty

36. Makes promises with no follow-through

37. Exhibits double standard of behavior/male supremacy

38. Fails to be truthful/honest

39. Is unable to trust or be trusted

40. Makes cruel/derogatory comments passed off as "teasing"

41. Displays cruelty to children/animals

42. Has current or past abusive/violent behavior

43. Had aggressive/delinquent behavior as a youth

44. Witnessed IPV as a child

45. Was physically/psychologically abused as a child

46. Minimizes abusive behavior and its effects on others

47. Has a pattern of instability/conflict in relationships

48. Plays the victim/seeks sympathy

49. Family/friends have concerns

50. Uses "playful" force during sex

51. Coerces sex, alcohol/drug use

52. Treats others disrespectfully

53. Displays anger about someone/something often

54. Blames others for his problems/feelings

55. Is unpredictable

56. Has unrealistic expectations

57. Exhibits controlling/manipulative behavior

58. Excuses/rationalizes/justifies behavior

59. Displays antisocial or borderline/narcissistic personality traits

60. Believes he is blameless

61. Believes rules/consequences don't apply to him

62. Takes financial advantage of partner

63. Has history of unemployment/getting fired

64. Seeks financial control over partner

65. Exhibits heavy drug/alcohol use

66. Is unwilling to make/keep commitments

67. Is frequently unfaithful

68. Displays attitudes accepting/justifying abuse

69. Exhibits cultural acceptance of violence

70. Displays hostility toward women

71. Has ongoing depression

72. Makes threats of suicide

73. Is secretive about past alluding to addictions/illegal behavior

74. Desires power and control in relationships

75. Gets what he wants one way or another

STARTING A NEW RELATIONSHIP: DO

<u>Do</u> feel confident in who you are.

<u>Do</u> meet in public places for the first several dates.

<u>Do</u> start with non-threatening activities.

<u>Do</u> share honestly about who you are and what you want in a relationship.

<u>Do</u> notice common interests.

<u>Do</u> ask about likes and dislikes.

<u>Do</u> ask about family, friends, and past relationships.

<u>Do</u> ask about values and beliefs.

<u>Do</u> ask about goals and dreams.

<u>Do</u> use caution when meeting people on the internet.

<u>Do</u> trust your instincts about being safe.

<u>Do</u> bring your own money and be prepared to pay.

<u>Do</u> take time to get to know each other well.

<u>Do</u> watch and listen for red flags.

<u>Do</u> use caution when introducing your new partner to your children.

<u>Do</u> ask trusted family and friends for their opinion of your partner.

<u>Do</u> tell someone who you'll be with and where you're going.

<u>Do</u> keep your boundaries in place.

STARTING A NEW RELATIONSHIP: DON'T

<u>Don't</u> play games; tell him if you are interested or not.

<u>Don't</u> get drunk or high to "loosen up" or feel confident on a date.

<u>Don't</u> get into a car alone or become isolated with people you don't know.

<u>Don't</u> go alone to other people's homes.

<u>Don't</u> invite people you just met to your home.

<u>Don't</u> introduce your new dating partner to your children too soon.

<u>Don't</u> leave your children alone with your new dating partner.

<u>Don't</u> monopolize the conversation talking about your ex.

<u>Don't</u> send mixed messages, especially about sex.

<u>Don't</u> do anything you don't want to do, including anything sexual.

<u>Don't</u> pretend to be someone you are not so he will like you.

<u>Don't</u> judge him based on your past relationships.

<u>Don't</u> share too much too fast.

RELATIONSHIP RIGHTS

1. I have the right to stay true to who God created me to be.

2. I have the right to continue to grow and change as a Christian and as a person.

3. I have the right to seek help, if needed, without being criticized for it.

4. I have the right to live free from all types of coercion, intimidation, violence, and abuse.

5. I have a right to healthy love and to be loved in a healthy manner.

6. I have a right to enjoy all the fruits of the spirit: love, joy, peace, patience, kindness, goodness, faithfulness, gentleness, and self-control. (Galatians 5: 22-23)

7. I have a right to be valued and respected.

8. I have a right to live without shame, blame, or guilt.

9. I have a right to feel and express my emotions.

10. I have a right to maintain [nonsexual] relationships apart from my partner.

11. I have the right to expect honesty and trust.

12. I have the right to express my opinions and have my opinions respected, even those that may differ from my partner's.

13. I have the right to pursue activities without my partner or to refuse to participate in activities I don't enjoy.

14. I have the right to have my decisions respected, even if I change my mind.

15. I have the right to set and enforce boundaries and to privacy.

16. I have the right to be imperfect.

17. I have the right to change my feelings toward someone.

18. I have the right to separate from unhealthy relationships.

CREATING HEALTHY BOUNDARIES

By setting healthy boundaries, we help ourselves and others understand the rules and expectations for a relationship or situation. The best time to set boundaries is before you need them.

STEP 1: **Describe the actions or behaviors you want or don't want.**

Example: I don't like lying.

STEP 2: **Describe the actions you will take to protect yourself.**

Example: I don't like lying.

If you lie to me, I will confront you about your lack of honesty.

If you lie to me, I'm going to need you to re-establish trust.

If you lie to me, I will be checking to see if future information you give me is true.

STEP 3: **Establish enforceable consequences for protecting your boundaries.**

Example: I don't like lying.

If you lie to me, I will confront you about your lack of honesty.

If you lie to me, I'm going to need you to re-establish trust.

If you lie to me, I will be checking to see if future information you give me is true.

If you continue lying to me, I will end our relationship.

If you continue lying to me, I'm not going to spend as much time with you.

Every time I know you are lying, I will leave/stop talking to you.

Healthy boundaries create healthy relationships.

*Underdeveloped boundaries attract those
who will take advantage of you.*

SETTING BOUNDARIES: GO-TO STATEMENTS

1. I'm sorry you feel that way.

2. I'm not comfortable/okay with that.

3. That doesn't work for me.

4. I need you to respect my boundaries.

5. I won't be doing that.

6. I don't agree.

7. I don't feel comfortable doing that.

8. It sounds as if you have a problem.

9. I won't be solving your problem.

10. I already have plans.

11. I'm not available.

12. I won't be participating/helping.

13. I need to think about what I want to do.

14. I won't give you an answer now.

15. I have to get this done.

16. Now is not a good time.

17. I'm not able to take that on right now.

18. My time is already committed.

19. I am unable to help at this time.

20. I'm unable to make that big of a commitment right now.

21. I don't feel comfortable discussing this.

22. I'm not going to discuss this with you.

23. I won't change my mind.

24. I need to honor my commitments to my family.

25. I've already answered that question.

26. I said, "No."

27. Please stop.

28. I have made my decision.

29. I respect your right to feel that way.

30. If that's what you feel you need to do.

31. I'm sticking to what I said.

32. Please say that in a different way.

33. You are violating my boundary.

34. Please stop disrespecting my wishes/decisions.

35. Talk to my attorney/the court.

36. I will follow the court order as it is written.

37. I won't be responding to your calls/texts/messages/emails.

38. That's not your decision to make.

39. I will make that decision.

40. I will ask for your help when I need it.

SAFETY PLANNING

SAFETY DURING AN ARGUMENT

- Stay in an area with an exit and avoid letting the other person get between you and the exit.

- Practice getting out of your home safely.

- Avoid rooms with weapons, such as the kitchen.

- Have emergency 911 phones hidden throughout the home.

- Tell trustworthy neighbors about the violence. Ask them to call the police if they hear or see any disturbance.

- Devise a code word or signal to use with your family, friends, coworkers, and trustworthy neighbors to indicate that you need the police.

- Do what you can to de-escalate the situation.

- Trust your instincts and judgment. You have the right to protect yourself until you are out of danger.

SAFETY WHEN PREPARING TO LEAVE

- Work with people you trust to help make your plans.

- Establish your independence. Open savings and credit card accounts in your name only and specifically instruct institutions that your partner is not to have access. Have personal mail sent to a different address.

- Keep your purse and keys readily accessible at all times.

- Leave money, extra keys, copies of important documents, extra medicine, and clothes with someone you trust so you can leave quickly.

- Review and rehearse your safety plan.

- Keep a packed bag at a trusted relative's or friend's home.

- Plan where you will go if you have to leave. Have a second location ready.

- Make arrangements for pets.

SAFETY IN YOUR OWN HOME

- Change the locks on your doors. (Landlords in many states are legally obligated to change locks within 24 hours if you are experiencing domestic violence.)

- Install or ask your landlord for increased security measures including locks and bars on your windows, replacing wooden doors with metal ones, additional locks for doors, installation of a security system, wedges for doors, etc.

- Devise escape routes from the second floor.

- Install smoke detectors and fire extinguishers on each level of the home.

- Discuss and practice a safety plan with your children for when you are not with them.

- Inform your children's schools or caregivers which people have permission to pick up your children.

- Inform trusted neighbors and your landlord that your partner no longer lives with you. Provide them with a picture of your partner and ask that they call the police if he is seen near your home.

- Teach your children how to call 911 or contact a safe person for help. Make sure they know the address.

- Position your vehicle in a way that allows for the quickest exit.

- Register with your state's Safe At Home program to protect your address.

SAFETY WITH A PROTECTION ORDER

- Keep your Protection Order or pictures of it with you at all times.

- Inform trusted family, friends, neighbors, coworkers, and health care providers that you have a Protection Order in effect.

- Give a copy to a trusted neighbor, friend or family member, and local law enforcement in areas you frequent.

- Give a copy to your children's schools or daycare.

- Call the police or file a police report if your abuser violates the Protection Order. Notify your attorney and others who have knowledge of your Order.

- Think of alternative ways to keep safe if the police do not respond right away.

- Document violations of the Protection Order. Include dates, times, what occurred, and any witnesses.

SAFETY ON THE JOB AND IN PUBLIC

- Decide whom at work you will inform of your situation (include building security).

- Provide a photo of your abuser for quick identification.

- Screen your telephone calls.

- Devise a safety plan for leaving work such as exiting through the back door.

- Have someone escort you when leaving and wait with you until you are safely en route.

- Use a variety of routes to go home from frequented places.

- Rehearse what you would do if something happened while going home, such as picking a safe place for yourself.

- Create a safety routine when you arrive home: checking your house and property, checking in with someone to let them know you are safe, etc.

SAFETY WITH TECHNOLOGY

- Use a phone to make or receive personal calls your partner cannot access, cannot access the billing records, or cannot change settings to track you.

- Use a computer your partner cannot access to seek help and resources.

- Arrange with government agencies, including the courts and mail service providers, to restrict access to your information.

- Change passwords on online accounts, including social media.

- Ask friends and family to refrain from giving out any information about you online.

- Find a trusted person familiar with technology to help you secure privacy and protection from any attempts by your partner to monitor your activities.

SAFETY AND YOUR EMOTIONAL HEALTH

- Identify whom you can rely on for emotional support. The National Domestic Violence Hotline number is (800) 799-SAFE (7233).

- Identify a trusted person you can call or spend time with before making decisions about returning to your partner.

- If you must communicate with your abuser, determine the safest way to do so and avoid being alone with him.

- Advocate for yourself and your needs. Find people and resources you can safely and openly talk to and ask for help. You are not alone, and you do not have to go through this by yourself.

- Look into counseling and support groups that directly address your experiences and needs.

- Find ways to care for yourself: exercise, make time to relax, create a safe environment, do things you enjoy, get as much support as you can.

INTERNET AND COMPUTER SAFETY

- Remember that all computer and online activity may be monitored.

- Abusers may monitor your emails and internet activity. If you are planning to flee to a particular location, don't look at classified ads for jobs and apartments, bus tickets, etc. for your destination.

- It is safer to use a computer in a public library, at a trusted friend's house, at an internet cafe, or any other public terminal.

- Abusers may also track your activity and whereabouts through your cell phone. If you think there a chance this may be happening, take your phone into your provider or someone familiar with spyware and have it thoroughly checked.

- If your phone has been compromised and you get a new one, do NOT update your phone using the cloud.

CHECKLIST: WHAT YOU SHOULD TAKE WHEN YOU LEAVE

LEGAL PAPERS
- Protection order/stalking order

- Lease, rental agreement, house deed

- Car registration and title

- Health and life insurance cards

- Divorce papers

- Custody papers

- Copies of police reports, photographs of injuries, and related medical records

IDENTIFICATION

- Driver's license
- Passports
- Birth certificates
- Social security cards
- Self-sufficiency/disability identification
- Medical insurance cards
- Medicare/Medicaid cards
- Immigration information

ADDITIONAL PAPERS

- Medical records for you and your children
- School and vaccination records
- Work permits/green cards
- VISA
- Marriage, divorce, or separation papers
- Car loan/payment information
- Insurance papers
- Recent bank statements
- Recent credit card statements
- Latest tax returns
- Lease, rental agreement, or house deed
- Mortgage payment information
- Proof of assets

OTHER

- House, work, and car keys
- Medications and medical supplies
- Cell phone and chargers

- Money, checkbook, bankbooks
- Debit, credit, and ATM cards
- Public assistance cards
- Valuables, photos, etc.
- Address book or written contact list
- Phone card/safety cell phone
- Clothes, security blankets, small toys for children
- Sentimental items
- Clothes, hygiene necessities, etc. for yourself
- Pictures of children
- Picture of partner
- Documentation of abuse including journals and photos

You are not alone!

National Domestic Violence Hotline:
(800) 799-SAFE (7233)

Notes

Notes

Notes

Notes

Notes

Notes

Notes

Notes

Notes

Notes

CPSIA information can be obtained
at www.ICGtesting.com
Printed in the USA
JSHW030210270921
19018JS00003B/5

9 781952 025495